Montana State Irrigation Convention

Report of the Proceedings of the State Irrigation Convention

Held in Electirc Hall in the City of Helena, Montana, on Thursday, Friday,

and Saturday, January 7, 8 and 9, 1892

Montana State Irrigation Convention

Report of the Proceedings of the State Irrigation Convention
Held in Electirc Hall in the City of Helena, Montana, on Thursday, Friday, and Saturday, January 7, 8 and 9, 1892

ISBN/EAN: 9783337185619

Printed in Europe, USA, Canada, Australia, Japan

Cover: Foto ©ninafisch / pixelio.de

More available books at **www.hansebooks.com**

REPORT

OF THE

PROCEEDINGS

OF THE

STATE IRRIGATION CONVEN[TION]

HELD IN ELECTRIC HAL[L]

IN THE

CITY OF HELENA,

ON

Thursday, Friday and [Saturday]

JANUARY 7, 8 AND [9]

WITH AN

APPENDI[X]

Showing the State of Irrigation in [Montana]

HELENA, MONT
INDEPENDENT PUBLISHING CO.
1892

REPORT

OF THE

PROCEEDINGS

OF THE

STATE IRRIGATION CONVENTION

HELD IN ELECTRIC HALL

IN THE

CITY OF HELENA, MONTANA,

ON

Thursday, Friday and Saturday,

JANUARY 7, 8 AND 9, 1892.

WITH AN

APPENDIX

Showing the State of Irrigation in the Counties.

HELENA, MONT.:
INDEPENDENT PUBLISHING CO.
1892

OFFICIAL REPORT.

Compiled by E. D. WEED, B. BROWN and W. C. CHILD, composing the Publication Committee.

CALL

FOR THE
STATE IRRIGATION CONVENTION.

WHEREAS, the Irrigation Congress which lately met at Salt Lake City, Utah, adopted the following platform:

Resolved, That this congress is in favor of granting in trust, upon such conditions as may serve the public interest, to the states and territories needful of irrigation, all lands now a part of the public domain within such states and territories, excepting mineral lands, for the purpose of developing irrigation, to render the lands now arid fertile and capable of supporting a population.

Resolved, That it is the sense of this convention that the committee selected to propose and present to Congress the memorial of this convention respecting public lands, should ask as a preliminary to the cession of all the lands in the territories in accordance with the resolutions of the convention, a liberal grant to said territories, and to the States to be formed therefrom, of the public lands to be devoted to public school purposes.

WHEREAS, Large areas of arid lands and semi-arid lands, situated upon the great plains in the Dakotas, western Nebraska, Kansas and Oklahoma were settled upon in good faith, by homeseekers, under the supposition that they were entering agricultural lands, and

WHEREAS, The settlers upon such lands have expended much time and money upon the same; and paid into the United States treasury therefor many millions of dollars, only to discover that irrigation, to a greater or less extent, is necessary in making homes for themselves thereon; therefore, be it

Resolved, That the representatives of all the states and territories directly interested in irrigation, do hereby pledge their unwavering support to the just demands of such settlers, that the general government shall donate at least a portion of the funds received from the sale of such lands toward the procurement of the means necessary for their irrigation.

Resolved, That this Congress heartily endorse the irrigation work of the agricultural department of the national government in the collection and dissemination of information; especially its admirable progress reports covering the whole field of irrigation development, and that it favors large appropriations for this work hereafter.

And whereas it is deemed advisable to obtain a direct expression of the people of this state npon the resolutions aforesaid, now therefore, for that purpose and to that end, a convention is hereby called to meet at the city of Helena, on Thursday, January 7, 1892, at 12 o'clock m. The apportionment of delegates has been made as follows: Beaverhead, 6; Choteau, 10; Custer, 4; Dawson, 2; Deer Lodge, 28; Fergus, 6; Gallatin, 8; Lewis and Clarke, 26; Meagher, 8; Missoula, 22; Madison, 8; Park, 10; Silver Bow, 40; Yellowstone, 5.

The Boards of County Commissioners of the several counties are earnestly requested to appoint delegates at their December meeting, according to the foregoing apportionment, based upon two delegates to each 300 voters. JOS. K. TOOLE,
Governor of Montana.

RESOLUTIONS

ADOPTED BY THE

MONTANA STATE IRRIGATION CONVENTION

Resolved, That in the judgment of this Convention it is the duty of the general government to aid in the development by irrigation of the arid lands in the several states and territories where such lands exist; and while we do not deem it desirable that the control and title of such lands should pass from the general government to the several States containing them, we do nevertheless urge at least that the proceeds arising from the sale of such lands shall be applied to the supply of water for their development for the purpose of agriculture, and we urge upon our Senators and Representatives in Congress to use every effort to accomplish such legislation as will bring about this desirable result, not only in our own State, but to all other States and Territories similarly situated.

Resolved, That it is the sense of this Convention that the committee selected to propose and present to Congress the memorial of this Convention respecting public lands, should ask in accordance with the resolutions of this Convention a liberal grant to said Territories and to the States to be formed therefrom of the public lands to be devoted to public school purposes.

WHEREAS, Large areas of arid lands and semi-arid lands, situated upon the great plains in the Dakotas, western Nebraska, Kansas and Oklahoma were settled upon in good faith, by home seekers, under the supposition that they were entering agricultural lands, and

WHEREAS, The settlers upon such lands have expended much time and money upon the same, and paid into the United States Treasury therefor many millions of dollars, only to discover that irrigation, to a greater or less extent, is necessary in making homes for themselves thereon; therefore be it

Resolved, That the Representatives of all the States and Territories directly interested in irrigation, do hereby pledge their unwavering support to the just demands of such settlers; that the general government shall donate at least a portion of the funds received from the sale of such lands toward the procurement of the means necessary for their irrigation.

WHEREAS, The Convention has heard with interest the reports from different parts of the State in reference to the matter of artesian wells now in active flow in different localities, therefore

Resolved, That this Convention earnestly urge upon our Senators and Representatives in Congress to use every effort to secure as large an appropriation as possible for the purpose of testing the question as to the practicability of this matter of water supply for this State, the money to be used in the actual sinking of wells, and not in expensive theorizing.

Resolved, That we believe it will best subserve the interests of this State if no appropriation whatever be made under the direction of Major Powell, of the government geological survey for the state of Montana. But we do ask for appropriation for scientific research under a State Department of Agriculture, whereby knowledge of much value to this State may be obtained and a complete check of all moneys expended be made.

REPORT OF PROCEEDINGS

OF THE

STATE IRRIGATION CONVENTION

Held at Helena, Montana, January, 8, 9, 10, 1892.

THURSDAY MORNING.

January 8, promptly at 11 o'clock A. M., ex-Governor S. T. Hauser called the State Irrigation Convention, assembled in answer to the call of Governor J. K. Toole, to order. He referred briefly to the objects of the Convention, and then introduced Lieutenant Governor J. K. Rickards, who welcomed the delegates to the State Capital on behalf of Governor Toole. The Lieutenant Governor said:

Mr. Chairman and Gentlemen of the Convention:

I am sure that we all very much regret that the Governor of the State is absent. As I said playfully this morning, it was he who acted as midwife of this Convention, and it would be eminently fit and proper that he should address you and welcome you to the Capital. It is, however, my pleasure to fill the Governor's place and welcome you. We have met at the call of our most worthy Governor to consider and discuss a subject which is filling to-day a large place in the minds of the people and is challenging the best thought of our ablest statesmen. I do not believe it is expecting too much of you to say that this Convention, made up as it is of the best citizens, will mark the opening of a new era in the development of our grand State.

I am proud to be a citizen of Montana. I enjoy very much seeing the coming together of such a body of men from all parts of the State, and I enjoy seeing them come together to discuss and deliberate upon such momentous questions as will come before you. I enjoy more than I can find words to express witnessing, on the eve of a great political struggle, men coming together, of all political complexions, not to discuss political questions, but each vieing with the other and actuated by public interests, to render the best service to this State. [Applause.] I have confidence in this body of my fellow citizens. You will remember that when Mr. Gould was before a Senate committee the question was asked him, "What are your politics?" Mr. Gould answered: "When I am in a Democratic district I am a Democrat; when I am in a Republican district I am a Republican, and when I am in a doubtful district I am doubtful, but I am always an Erie man." So that I say I have confidence in this body, for you would not have come here at the call of the Chief Magistrate if you were not first and all the time Montanians. [Loud applause.]

Now, I think you all appreciate the magnitude of the questions that will come before you and the object of this Convention. It is not my purpose to attempt any discussion of the subject. I am sure, however, that in deliberating you will forget all partisan discussion, and that there will be a unanimity of purpose to advance the material interests of the grand State of Montana.

Now, I believe it is expected of me to speak a few words of welcome. I scarcely know how to do this. However, I will say that inasmuch as the excellent and popular Mayor of the city has turned over the keys of the city, so it is fit and proper for me to turn over the keys of the Executive Mansion and Capitol buildings—that is if you can find them. [Loud laughter and applause.] And in the true Western style elevate your feet on the table. There are no cuspidores on the floor to embarrass you. If I could, I would like to turn over to you the combination of the State Treasury safe, but the State Treasurer is an excellent and good-natured gentleman, who will do anything he can for you. Now, in behalf of the great State of Montana, of which we are all proud citizens, I welcome you to the Capital, and invoke for you at the close of your deliberations the verdict of well done from a grateful constituency. I say, again, welcome.

At the conclusion of the Lieutenant Governor's address the Chairman introduced Mayor T. H. Kleinschmidt, who extended to the delegates the freedom of the city in the following language:

Mr. Chairman and Gentlemen of the Irrigation Convention:

It is not often in the history of one so situated as myself to have the privilege of extending a welcome to a city of which we are residents. I extend a hearty welcome to you, gentlemen, and can add but very little to that which has been said by the Lieutenant Governor on the subject for which you are assembled, a question vital to the interests of this State. If we look about us over this vast territory that only requires the labor of husbandry to make it productive, and more productive than any other state, we can appreciate the task of this Congress to develop and submit something for the people for them to act on, and for the benefit to be derived from such action. I say it is a proud privilege to extend to you a hearty welcome to our city. The Lieutenant Governor says he will turn over the keys if you can find the Capitol buildings. I will go farther. This city has no keys; the gates are wide open.

W. A. Clark, of Silver Bow: I assume that the first appropriate action of this Convention will be to affect a temporary organization, and probably the appointment of some committees. If I am correct in this I will take the liberty and the pleasure of placing in nomination as temporary chairman of this Convention, Hon. S. T. Hauser.

Mr. Clark put the vote and declared Mr. Hauser duly elected as temporary chairman.

Mr. Hauser: Gentlemen of the Convention, I thank you for the compliment and honor, and I am at your service.

On motion George W. Irvine II., of Silver Bow, was elected temporary secretary.

The Chairman: I expected to be made temporary chairman, and called on Mr. Irvine, who promised to make a speech for me.

The Chairman then introduced Mr. Irvine, who said:

Mr. Chairman and Gentlemen of the Convention:

Governor Hauser has been treating me a little unfair. I can recall no conversation of the kind. I want to say to you that in an irrigation convention I am not well equipped. I have noticed in life that every single possible quantity or atom of organization has life. I have pursued my investigation to an extent that I have found there is life in the plant, there is life in the shrub, there is life in the tree, there is life in every portion of the earth. All that's required is that it be called into actual existence. I believe the serious business of this convention is one of the greatest importance. Our people from our side of the Rocky Mountains have come over as lay members rather than as active members. We come here desiring to learn and to make such recommendations as shall present themselves. Of course in coming to this Convention we believe in the outline of the Salt Lake platform, probably differing in some details. The manner of the control of the lands and their disposal to corporations and individuals is all a matter of details. The turning over of the lands to the State involves a number of collateral questions. We have the question of cutting timber on the public domain. It is relative to this question. So with the forestry problem. We don't want this matter relegated to the keeping of a few gentlemen in the East who base their knowledge of the subject upon the reports of agents, who don't know the tamarack monarch of the forest from an ordinary bull pine. I say candidly that the question of the control of the forests should also be turned over to the State. Therefore we are interested in getting their control, and I think we can do it better than those who are assuming to care for the American forests.

On motion of John W. Thompson, of Lewis and Clarke county, the following committee on credentials was appointed:

J. M. Patterson—Choteau.
J. A. Harris—Cascade.
W. B. S. Higgins—Custer.
J. C. Auld—Dawson.
Peter Levengood—Deer Lodge.
E. G. Brooke—Jefferson.
J. A. Browne—Beaverhead.
B. F. Shuart—Yellowstone.
O. C. Cooper—Missoula.
W. H. Sutherlin—Meagher.
R. O. Hickman—Madison.
W. A. Harrison—Park.
B. F. Leggett—Silver Bow.
A. L. Corbley—Gallatin.
E. D. Weed—Lewis and Clark.
H. L. Fisher—Fergus.

An adjournment was taken till 2 o'clock p. m.

THURSDAY AFTERNOON.

Promptly at 2 o'clock Chairman Hauser called the Convention to order. Chairman E. D. Weed, of the credentials committee, reported the following delegates entitled to seats:

Beaverhead—H. R. Melton, A. Eliel, Thomas M. Selwey, W. C. Orr, John C. Brenner, J. A. Browne.

Custer—Sam Gordon, A. M. Cree, W. B. S. Higgins, J. W. Strevell.

Choteau—Thomas C. Burns, Z. T. Burton, J. F. Patterson, J. W. Power.

Cascade—Maurice S. Parker, S. B. Robbins, George E. Ingersoll, E. D. Hastie, John M. Castner, John F. Wegner, John W. McKnight, John A. Harris, H. P. Rolfe, N. T. Porter.

Dawson—Jas. G. Ramsay, J. C. Auld.

Deer Lodge—T. C. Davidson, Allen Kimmerly, Peter Levengood, J. Stuckey, Jno. R. Quigley, P. Jensen, J. Richey, P. Valiton, Byron Wood, W. A. Hansley, C. Hardenbrook, N. J. Beilenberg, D. Berry,

Jos. Gough, J. W. Blair, M. Geary, G. W. Morse, W. Dingwall, Wm. Wallace, Jno. Fetherman, W. T. Elliott, John Gandell, F. M. Durfee, B. Parrott, Wm. Morton, I. Gibbs, C. F. Mussigbrod, E. Girard.

Gallatin—Walter Cooper, J. W. Caldwell, William Flannery, O. P. Chisholm, W. W. Alderson, Chas. A. Gregory, A. L. Corbly, H. H. Sappington.

Fergus—C. W. Baylies, H. L. Fisher, C. M. Goodell, James Ettien, David Hilger and C. V. Peck.

Jefferson—Ed Cardwell, G. Ryan, E. G. Brooke, A. L. Love, John Murray, J. I. Winslow, J. Patterson, A. H. Moulton, B. Townsley, W. C. Whaley.

Lewis and Clarke—S. T. Hauser, S. Word, W. B. Hundley, J. T. Murphy, T. H. Kleinschmidt, H. M. Parchen, W. E. Cullen, D. S. Wade, D. A. Cory, J. H. Longmaid, J. B. Clayberg, A. M. Holter, John W. Thompson, E. D. Weed, J. W. Wade, Donald Bradford, A. J. Seligman, A. J. Burns, E. Beach, A. C. Botkin, A. G. Lombard, Abraham Thomas, R. H. Howey, W. C. Child, F. P. Sterling.

Meagher—J. B. Stafford, C. W. Cook, H. Whaley, J. E. Knnouse, W. H. Sutherlin, N. E. Benson, R. H. Clendenin, W. Brady.

Missoula—John E. Cyr, G. Deschamps, Mose Clemens, Peter Schaffer, A. A. Pourier, A. G. England, M. Flyn, W. J. Brennan, W. R. Ramsdell, Lyman Loring, A. W. Twaney, J. M. Eastland, E. M. Ratcliff, O. C. Cooper, R. A. O'Hara, G W. Ward, J. R. Faulds, J. S. Robertson, J. L. Hunter, S. Maclay, J. H. Mills, Frank Borroughs.

Madison—James W. Page, Patrick Carney, H. C. Harrison, A. W. Tanner, M. D. Jeffers, A. Metzel, M. Howes, R. O. Hickman.

Park—James Vestal, C. C. Day, W. A. Harrison, J. F. Work, James Smith, Samuel Bundock, J. L. DeHart, A. Myers.

Silver Bow—D. A. Morrison, Wm. Bowe, Jos. S. Harper, J. Carter, Thos. Couch, J. R. Boyce, Jr., S. F. Fletchett, C. A. Small, T. C. Jackson, J. McCauley, W. A. Ralston, P. A. Largey, Thos. O. Miles, Earnest Spear, E. Gregson, H. H. Eccleston, Levi Cartier, L. G. Wunderlich, Wm. Stolte, Chas. H. Carver, Simon Hauswirth, W. A. Clark, Geo. H. Casey, John A. Leggatt, Napoleon Geneveaux, C. S. Baxter, Wm. Hamilton, Lee W. Foster, T. M: Robbins, David S. Durey, Geo. H. Tong, J. G. Maddox, T. C. Miles, J. H. McQueeney, J. J. Feeley, J. F. Cowan, Wm. Woodward, C. L. Bauman, Geo. W. Irvine, H.

Yellowstone—B. F. Shuart, Olney Taylor, Charles A. Wenstrum, R. J. Martin.

The report was adopted and the committee was made permanent.

There was a call for Senator T. C. Power, who said:

Mr. Chairman and Gentlemen of the Convention:

This is not the time to make any speeches. I believe you have assembled from all parts of the State for the purpose of investigating this great question of irrigation in this State, and I will not delay you at this time with any speech; but after you proceed with business, and want to ask any questions about government aid, I will be glad to answer them, and I will be in readiness to do that to the best of my ability. I know that members are here from the farming sections who want to return as soon as possible, and I would ask that we despatch our business as quickly as possible. On that account I am not going to say anything further just now.

On motion the following Committee on Permanent Organization and Order of Business was appointed:

Adolph Eliel—Beaverhead.
John W. Power—Choteau.
J. C. Auld—Dawson.
James Ettien—Fergus.
Edward Cardwell—Jefferson.
Patrick Carney—Madison.
A. L. England—Missoula.
J. H. McQueeney—Silver Bow.
A. M. Cree—Custer.
E. D. Hastie—Cascade.
G. W. Morris—Deer Lodge.
Charles A. Gregory—Gallatin.
W. B. Hundley—Lewis and Clarke.
J. B. Stafford—Meagher.
Alfred Myers—Park.
Olney Taylor—Yellowstone.

On motion of Mr. Botkin, of Lewis and Clarke, a recess of thirty minutes was taken in order to give the Committee on Permanent Organization and Order of Business time to report.

The report of the committee, submitted by Chairman Alfred Myers and read by Secretary C. A. Gregory, was as follows:

Gentlemen of the Convention:

Your Committee on Permanent Organization and Order of Business beg leave to report as follows:

Samuel T. Hauser, of Lewis and Clarke, President.
C. E. Ingersoll, of Cascade, Secretary.
George H. Casey, of Silver Bow, Assistant Secretary.
S. Alexander, Sergeant at Arms.
Morris Langhorne and Eddy Boos, Pages.

Order of Business—First, election of officers; second, reading of the call for this Convention; third, presentation of resolutions.

We recommend that all resolutions presented to this Convention shall be in writing, and that the same shall be referred to the Committee on Resolutions without debate. We also recommend that each county appoint one of its delegates to report to this Convention the state of irrigation in his respective county. These reports to be made on the floor of this house. And your Committee further recommend that for rules this Convention shall be governed by the permanent rules of the House of Representatives of the Second session of the Legislature of the State of Montana. All of which is respectfully submitted.   A. MEYERS, Chairman.

CHARLES A. GREGORY, Secretary.

Mr. Botkin, of Lewis and Clarke, moved to amend the report by striking out that portion of it recommending that resolutions introduced be referred to the Committee on Resolutions without discussion.

The Chairman of the Committee said that it was the opinion of the Committee that resolutions should be referred to the Committee on Resolutions for action, and that discussion of them would follow after the report of the Committee had been made to the Convention.

Mr. Botkin: It would be well if they could be referred to the Committee on Resolutions for presentation, but not if they are to be referred to the Committee on Resolutions for suppression, and that is very apt to be their fate. I hold that each resolution should be fairly discussed. [Applause.]

The motion on the amendment was put by the Chairman and carried.

Mr. Meyers: I move to amend the report by making George W. Irvin II., of Silver Bow, Vice President of this Convention. Seconded and unanimously carried.

The report of the Committee as amended was unanimously adopted.

A motion was adopted that a Committee on Resolutions, consisting of one member from each county, be constituted, to be selected by the Chairman of each delegation. The following were named as members of the Committee:

H. R. Melton—Beaverhead.
M. S. Parker—Cascade.
James R. Ramsey—Dawson.
Clarence Goodall—Fergus.
O. L. Love—Jefferson.
A. W. Tanner—Madison.
R. E. O'Hara—Missoula.
W. A. Clark—Silver Bow.
Samuel Gordon—Custer.
Z. T. Burton—Choteau.
N. J. Beilenberg—Deer Lodge.
O. P. Chisholm - Gallatin.
A C. Botkin—Lewis and Clarke.
W. H. Sutherlin—Meagher.
J. L. De Hart—Park.
B. F. Shuart—Yellowstone.

There was a call for Chairman Hauser to make a speech on his election as permanent chairman, and in reply he said:

Gentlemen of the Convention:

I certainly appreciate the high honor, and also the importance of this Convention When I was asked to call the Convention to order by our absent Governor I particularly requested that I should be allowed about two or three hours to make a speech. He did not think I should occupy the attention of the Convention that long. With that understanding I consented to act as temporary chairman. At first I did not take much interest in this question. I have paid as high as 40 cents an inch for water during the last ten or fifteen years, and higher than that for other irrigants. But I find it is a better plan to stand by water. If we stand by this subject we will awaken an interest in the people of the east. We have stood by them for years in their appropriations of millions, and there is no reason why we should not get these lands. When this question was broached to me in making me temporary chairman, I had not taken much thought of it. My interests had been in mining, cattle and sheep. I thought it perfectly ridiculous to subscribe toward the Helena artesian well fund. The facts are that when you measure the water in the Prickly Pear Valley flowing to waste in the months of June and July, there is enough to irrigate this entire valley. I had not paid any attention to irrigation up to this time. I did not think there was anything in it, but the time will come when we will all think so. I believe this is the most important question raised in any country. There are lands in the Prickly Pear valley that without water, if sold by the sheriff, would not be worth $5 per acre. With water on them they are worth from $50 to $75 per acre.

There seems to be some disposition among those who differ in politics with me - like my friend Power, for instance – not to take these lands. I have been in Montana too long for that. If anybody is going to give me anything, I am going to take it. Montana men know how to take care of themselves.

On taking his seat next to the Chairman, as Vice Chairman, Mr. Irvine, of Silver Bow, said: "I am very much gratified at the compliment paid me. I do not consider that I have any particular intelligence that can go very far toward enlightening the gentlemen before me, and I think, if speech is silver, silence is golden, I will take the liberty of sitting down. After the eloquence of the Chairman I am certainly silenced for once in my life."

A. J. Seligman, of Lewis and Clarke: In order to bring the matter to a focus I will move that each county be entitled to the entire number of votes that the apportionment calls for, and that the majority of that county cast the votes of the absentees.

Z. T. Burton, of Choteau: I believe this Convention was called under certain rules directed to the boards of county commissioners, this Convention having been called by the Governor. It seems to me it would be arrogating authority to ourselves by making delegates who had never been chosen by the Commissioners.

Mr. Leggatt, of Silver Bow: In calling the roll I noticed one county had but one delegate here. It would be unfair for Dawson county, which has the largest interest in this matter, to be represented by one man. I therefore second the motion that each county be entitled to its full quota.

R. O. Hickman, of Madison: The gentleman from Silver Bow speaks of Dawson County. Mr. Ramsey has been selected as a delegate with Mr. Auld.

Mr. Botkin sent the following resolution to the Secretary's desk:

Resolved, That it is the sense of this Convention that reservoirs, canals, ditches and other works of irrigation, in case such policy is permitted by the Constitution, be taxed not on the cost or appraised valuation, but upon the income actually received from the sales of water.

R. H. Howey, of Lewis and Clarke: It occurs to me that is a proposition I would like to hear from some one on who is conversant with the proposition, giving the reasons for its adoption; or it ought perhaps be referred to the Committee on Resolutions.

Mr. Botkin: I would be very glad, as a member of the Committee on Resolutions, to hear some expression from the Convention.

Mr. Melton, of Beaverhead: If there is anything I am opposed to in this matter it is haste. I am inclined to be in favor of the resolution. I am not yet able to catch the full meaning of that resolution. I believe it should be turned over to the Committee on Resolutions. Let us go slow in this matter; let us do what we do intelligently, and then we will not regret it or do it over again.

Mr. Word, of Lewis and Clarke: I move that the resolution be made a special order at 10 o'clock to-morrow morning.

Mr. Weed: The Convention would like to hear from the author of the resolution.

Mr. Botkin: Mr. President, I beg leave to submit that I am peculiarly unfitted to express any conviction about the policy. It is because I sought knowledge and not to impart it that I introduced the resolution. The policy suggests itself to me as one wholly to be desired. It seems to me that a man who invests large sums of money in irrigation should not be taxed until those investments should have become fruitful. I can hardly see how we can invite capital to engage in enterprises of this character if taxation shall commence before the earning.

R. H. Howey: That is one side of that proposition, but it strikes me that there might be another side to it. The poor fellow who takes up a desert land claim is not exempt. If you exempt one side why not exempt the other? I think it would be a fair proposition to include the other side; to include the poor fellows on the homesteads.

W. A. Clark: I have simply one word to say on the proposition. I believe in encouraging by every legitimate means all kinds of enterprises in this State that will help to build it up, but I do not see how it would be or could be done equitably, to pass any legislation that would discriminate particularly in favor of any particular enterprise. Of course in anything like mining, which might be termed, in the language of insurance people, "extra hazardous," there might be some exceptions, and I believe that has been incorporated in the Constitution of this State. But so far as irrigation, perhaps, is concerned, I believe before entering upon any enterprises of this character we ought to calculate the chances of success, and not discriminate in favor of monopolists. I beg to suggest that it would be in conflict with the Constitution of Montana for the Legislature to make any exception of this character. The Constitution says that property of every character shall be taxed its full value. Legislation of this kind cannot be had until the Constitution shall be first amended.

Mr. Burton: There should be in my opinion no conflict between gentlemen largely interested in the mining industry and gentlemen who are interested in building irrigation canals and reservoirs. If the Constitution of this State, as it wisely did, looked upon the development of mining property as largely speculative, in what view can it be said that a man who erects large irrigation enterprises does not invest his money in works which are largely of a speculative character? As a constitutional question we cannot determine it, but as the sense of this Convention we can determine it. I believe a canal should be taxed according to the value placed on it, but its actual value to be determined from the sale of its water.

John W. Thompson, of Lewis and Clarke: I heartily agree with Mr. Burton. Permit me to say that there are men on the floor of this Convention who have invested largely in irrigation enterprises who will have to wait some years before they derive any revenue from them. Why should we be taxed until we have a revenue?

A. M. Holter, of Lewis and Clarke: This resolution should go to the Committee on Resolutions, and let them take time to consider it in regard to the taxation. On the constitutional question I want to say that a canal or ditch is simply a right of way, the same as a road. The Constitution does not make any provision for assessing roads or highways. I move that this resolution be referred to the Committee on Resolutions and be disposed of to-morrow.

The motion was put and carried.

Mr. Strevell, of Custer: I desire to make a suggestion. I have prepared a resolution, but I will premise it with a few remarks. The Governor in calling this Convention called it for the purpose of considering the action taken by another Convention at Salt Lake City, and it seems to me that it is desirable to confine ourselves to the business for which the Governor called this Convention; to bring that business before the Convention at the earliest moment. If I remember the call, the Governor has suggested to the Convention whether it would adopt the course taken at Salt Lake. Now, it is desirable to bring that call before this Convention. It is in the nature of an address to a legislature. I move that the call be referred to the Committee on Resolutions, to report at the earliest practicable moment, to bring before the Convention the main purpose. I think I am justified in asking this. The question is whether we will or will not ratify the action of the Salt Lake Convention.

The motion was put and carried.

Mr. Donald Bradford offered the following:

WHEREAS, Montana contains 93,349,200 acres; 38,000,000 acres comprise our ranges. Interspersed with these are 30,000,000 acres of farming lands, and

WHEREAS, Montana has limitless latent wealth, the fact must be recognized that we are face to face with a vast problem, that we must prepare now to solve and not procrastinate till too late to properly and economically master it, and

WHEREAS, It is fair to assume 15,000,000 acres to be the area subject to all practicable means of irrigation. Fifteen million acres, properly watered, means 1,000,000 additional rural population. Canals for 1,000,000 population mean, not alone irrigation, but demands for water power, for manufactories, water for houses, for cities and villages, and consequently a well balanced law prepared in the light of the experience of the countries of Europe, of Egypt and of India, that have, in a measure, overcome the difficulties in the proper distribution of water; a law anticipating the need of reservoir sites in every locality possessing irrigable lands, to prevent their occupancy and ultimate enlarged outlay in condemnation; a law that will place under the control of each district or drainage area their water supply, and will reduce the cost to a minimum; that will prevent discrimination as between landholders, and

WHEREAS, The constitutional life of the Legislature will not permit of an investigation or the research the importance of the subject demands, therefore be it

Resolved, By the Convention, constituting representatives from different portions of the State, that a committee of one from each county be appointed by the President of this Convention with power to prepare a bill and present it to the next legislature, which bill shall embody the following general points, to-wit: The creation of a State Irrigation and Immigration Commission, which shall be appointed by the Governor, together with a State Engineer, which Commission shall have power, through the State Engineer, to divide the State into districts, according to natural slopes; to prepare plans for the construction of the necessary canals and reservoirs or other works of any district; to have sole control of the construction; to cause the organization of any such district by the election by the legal voters of such district of five trustees, who shall exercise control of such canal, reservoir or other work of construction; issue bonds of such district for construction; levy taxes and otherwise provide for sinking fund, interest and repairs, subject in all cases to the laws of the State.

Mr. Bradford, in support of his resolution, said:

Mr. President:

I have prepared and introduced these resolutions with a view to crystalizing to some extent, and bringing before this body the question how the arid lands of Montana are to be made habitable for the accommodation of a vast population. In considering the best method of accomplishing this object, we should try to realize the work, not only this Convention and the next Legislature, but this epoch has mapped out for its achievement by the demands of civilization. We should bring home to our minds the fact that the public domain, in the rain belt, has practically become exhausted; that the so-called arid region, known in early days as the "Great American Desert," is the last resort as a relief for the millions of population annually flowing into the United States; that the eastern States are in a constant state of gestation and of delivery; that these youths are seeking outlets for their ambition, and that the Rocky Mountains, the arid region, the land of gold and silver, is the Mecca toward which they all turn their hopes. Therefore, I say, we must impress upon our minds the grandeur of the responsibility resting upon this Convention, of creating for this influx of humanity an avenue through which it may quickly utilize its energy.

There are several plans extant that attempt to cover the ground, but, according to my judgment, are seriously defective in the most vital requisites. First, the question arises, shall the national or state governments exercise general supervision? Second, if either, shall the ownership be by private corporations and individuals, with State supervisors, as in Colorado; State ownership and control, as in India; ownership by the people in districts through a board of directors that exercise absolute control, without any higher supervision, as in California; or the plan proposed in the resolutions, of district ownership and control with ultimate supervision both in construction and during operation by a permanent and competent State board or commission.

I will attempt to discuss each scheme as it is here presented: First—National control and perhaps construction is impracticable for the reason that it is too vast for comprehensive supervision by one man or one board of the minutia of each individual enterprise in the whole arid region—comprising Montana, Idaho, Washington, Oregon, California, the Dakotas, Wyoming, Colorado, Nebraska, Kansas, Utah, Arizona, Texas and New Mexico, containing 150,000,000 acres of irrigable and 500,000,000 acres of grazing lands. Second—It gives too much power to the central government through patronage. Third—It would be a tax upon States in no way benefitted. Fourth— The management would likely prove incompetent in that political favoritism would soon be the basis of all appointments and the people would have no remedy.

Fifth—Irrigation is essentially a local question that should be governed from its inception by local powers. Sixth—Irrigation securities will gain comparatively little through government guaranty—as under the plan proposed in the resolutions—the security would be so ably proven by a competent State Commission, aided by a State Engineer, that no question of the feasibility of any enterprise would arise. Seventh—The argument that the national government should control because of any inter-state complications that may arise is unsound, for the reason that the United States courts have jurisdiction over all litigation between States and the citizens of the several States. The same courts would, under the national plan, adjudicate all disputes arising from the use of water from a stream penetrating two or more States.

The Colorado plan can be diposed of by the statement of the simple fact that to set up a barrier between life and the means of sustaining life is an unnatural condition, and therefore would not be tolerated for a long period by the people, notwithstanding the fact that the State controls. The fact that a corporation has the fee-simple in the water or the means of distribution and declares division of profits from the proceeds of sale is sufficient reason why corporations should not exist. The further fact that nature decrees the use of irrigation is an unanswerable argument against a monopoly of the distribution of water.

India is a congregation of ignorance, poverty and slavery that, not being blessed by comparatively universal civilization as is here exemplified, could not, through a popular vote of the masses, provide for an intelligent system of irrigation other than by imperial management.

Irrigation in California is regulated by the law known as the "Wright law," whereby fifty or more holders of title, or evidence of title, to lands susceptible of one mode of irrigation from a common source and by the same system of works, may petition the county supervisors to cause the organization of a district according to the details prescribed under the law which provides for the election of a district board of directors, which board has the power to construct canals or other works, issue bonds, assess property through a district assessor, sit as a board of equalization, and in all respects regulate the affairs pertaining to irrigation in the district.

Should the area called for in the petition extend into two or more counties, the supervisors of the county within which the petition originated shall notify the supervisors of the other counties within whose boundaries the district extends of the fact that such district is organized, and such other supervisors are enjoined from interfering with or overlapping such district boundaries with any other district boundaries.

The defects in this law are so apparent it is necessary only to mention them in comparison with the plan proposed in the resolutions to show that while the California law is a decided step in advance and is the best existing law, it is far from being what it should be. It will be noted that a district may extend into two or more counties; that the district is established by the supervisors of one without the necessary co-operation of the other boards, wherein lies a foundation for conflict between the counties. The plan proposed in the resolutions would obviate this fault by giving to a central state commission the power to fix the boundaries of a district, to regulate its organization and to pass upon all disputes as between districts—counties as such having no jurisdiction. The California law gives to the board of county supervisors and to the board of directors of a district the sole power of deciding upon the feasibility of a scheme of irrigation.

Such boards, from the nature of things (their members not being as a rule engineers), are incompetent to judge of the practicability of a project; more than likely they would employ a local engineer with little or no experience, and, too, local bias would probably affect a board composed necessarily of farmers whose interests would demand the construction of works and the expenditure of money in the purchase of products of the farm. This plan is met in the proposed law by the creation of a state commission, which would be made up of engineers of known ability, with an engineering department thoroughly fortified with all data bearing upon the drainage and lands of the whole State—the number of acres susceptible of irrigation and the supply of water permanently available under all circumstances; the cost of construction of the necessary works and the size and class of work most suitable. I have been informed that out of $24,000,000 in bonds issued under the California law only $5,000,000 have been sold, leaving $19,000,000 unsold, caused, in my judgment, wholly by the lack of faith in the ability and honor of local boards. Without the confidence of the financial world in our securities it is heedless to attempt the reclamation of this empire of Montana.

This proposed law contemplates the management of immigration to the State. Through state management immigration would be under absolute control, as any tract of lands could be reclaimed and systematically settled by any class desired, through colonies or by individuals. All settlers would secure employment upon public works in course of construction for one or two years, thus aiding in building up each locality; in the meanwhile farms would be tilled, houses and fences erected, and prosperity would reign by the time water could be delivered. In addition it will place in circulation millions of dollars that will be repaid by its own results.

The State will soon reap the full fruition of such wise legislation by all such lands becoming subject to tax. Not alone will Montana gain by the immediate output of these lands—the population thus enhanced will create a growing demand for manufactories, woolen mills, iron furnaces, flouring mills, sugar and cheese factories and creameries and the innumerable accessories of such industries will spring up and add to the prosperity of our commonwealth. Railroads run by electricity, generated under the pressure of our mountain streams, will penetrate every section, and Montana will lead not alone in mineral, but in the production of every other source of wealth. I have in my possession the laws of every country practicing irrigation, and I believe that a law carrying out the ideas as expressed in the resolutions, as offered, will prove efficacious in every emergency, as it will embody the best parts of all, and will avoid the errors as well. The people now own the water in some states; they should own it in all and exercise ownership over the means of distribution. In this way only can conflicts be avoided and much litigation prevented.

On motion the resolution of Mr. Bradford was referred to the Committee on Resolutions.

On motion of Mr. Irvine, of Silver Bow, the press was invited to publish the resolution and argument of Mr. Bradford in full.

Mr. Leggatt, of Silver Bow, moved that the rules be suspended, and that all resolutions be referred to the Committee on Resolutions without debate. The motion was lost.

Adjourned until 10 A. M., January 8, 1892.

FRIDAY MORNING, JANUARY 8.

The Convention was called to order at 10 o'clock Friday morning by Chairman Hauser.

Samuel Word, in a short speech, called attention to the fact that the day was the anniversary of the birth of Andrew Jackson.

Senator Power: I would say to the Convention that we are very much obliged to the gentleman from Lewis and Clarke for putting us in mind of what has been done, but the question before us is what we want to heed. Keep your eyes open. We do not want our attention diverted just now. What we want to do is to keep our powder dry and our eyes on the guns. I will now ask for the report of the Committee on Resolutions.

The Secretary read as follows:

Hon. S. T. Hauser, President of the Irrigation Convention:

The Committee on Resolutions beg leave to make the following report: The platform of the Salt Lake Convention, after due consideration, is referred back to this Convention without recommendation, further than that said platform be referred to the committee of the whole for discussion.

W. A. CLARK, Chairman.

Mr. Strevell, of Custer: I move that the report be received and adopted.

Mr. Word, of Lewis and Clarke: I move to amend by receiving it and lay the report on the table for the action of this Convention without being adopted.

A. J. Seligman, of Lewis and Clarke: Will you kindly state what effect it will have as amended?

Mr. Word: Simply to lay on the table, to be called up at any time by any member. It is there for the action of the Convention. Possibly it can be taken up in committee of the whole as a special order. It is on the table subject to the call of the Convention.

Mr. Strevell, of Custer: If the report is immediately adopted, it will bring the matter before the Convention—the action of the Salt Lake Convention. I hope the amendment will not prevail.

Mr. Word: I withdraw my amendment.

Senator Power: I understand the business before the Convention is whether it will adopt the Salt Lake platform, which means segregation.

Mr. Strevell: I beg your pardon; that is not it at all.

The Chairman: I think the Senator is out of order.

Senator Power: I will give up the floor.

The motion of Mr. Strevell was put and carried.

Mr. Clark, of Silver Bow: I move that the Convention resolve itself into committee of the whole for the consideration of the Salt Lake platform.

The motion was put and carried. The President called Mr. Chisholm of Gallatin County to the chair.

IN COMMITTEE OF THE WHOLE.

The Chairman: We are now in committee of the whole for the discussion of the Salt Lake platform.

Mr. Strevell, of Custer: I move that the resolutions embracing the action of the Salt Lake Convention be taken up seriatim. The main point for discussion in this Convention will be raised upon the resolutions. I move that they be taken up in order.

On motion of John W. Thompson the Secretary read the call of the Governor for the Convention.

The Chairman: The Secretary will now read the first section of the resolutions of the Salt Lake Convention.

The Secretary read as follows:

Resolved, That this Congress is in favor of granting in trust, upon such conditions as may serve the public interest, to the states and territories needful of irrigation, all lands now a part of the public domain within such states and territories, excepting mineral lands, for the purpose of developing irrigation, to render the lands now arid fertile and capable of supporting a population.

The Chairman recognized Senator Power, who said:

Mr. Chairman and Gentlemen of the Convention:

I am not going to take up your time by making any remarks on this section, but on the subject from its beginning, from its incipiency, to the present, if that is in order. You have heard the resolution, sugar-coated, or you can read it in the proceedings of the Irrigation Congress at Salt Lake, the crystalization of their action, which is to cede these lands to the states absolutely, save and except mining lands. This action of the Salt Lake Congress was preconceived and prearranged before that Congress met. The delegates from this State, and I believe they will not deny the assertion, did not understand the situation. Gentlemen who represented this State at the Salt Lake Irrigation Congress will appear before you to-day and speak on this proposition. These gentlemen did not understand that a deep and concocted plan had been laid. I did not understand its drift until told by some friends of irrigation measures. Having been warned, I watched some of the Senators that had made this a study. I wanted to know why they were so deeply interested, and saw afterwards that it was for the centralization of power, the increasing of their political holdings. I refer more particularly to the Senators from Wyoming. At the organization of the Senate, I thought I saw this cropping out. I asked to be put on the Irrigation Committee. They said they would see. A committee of seven was named to select members for the different Senate Committees. I found I was left out; but prior to it, I was asked how I felt about segregation. I said it was winter and we might want to ask the old man for something. I was referring to appropriations. This remark did not suit them. That Committee on Irrigation and Reclamation of Arid Lands is formed with Senator Warren as chairman. The others, outside of the chairman of the Committee on Railroads, are chiefly lawyers. I tried to convince that committee of seven that I was interested in irrigation; that I went to Dakota in 1860, when crops could not be raised, and where they now raise millions of bushels. I thought I understood the subject. No, sir; there was no place for me, because I did not absolutely fall into this trap. Now follow up the work. Governor Thomas of Utah issued his call. The outcome of that work you will see later. Then came the recommendation of Governor Toole; then the organization of this Convention. When we wanted to get a chairman, Mr. Clark was spoken of. We wanted to make him chairman, but he was committed to this question. We took chances on Governor Hauser, and lo, and behold, he is committed. Now, I say, keep your eyes open and look out. You will be asked to remain here a week if this, the endorsing of the Salt Lake programme, cannot be accomplished. I say, meet the issue; vote direct; say whether you want the lands ceded to the State or not. If you do desire segregation, you, in my opinion, oppose all appropriations from the government.

There are perhaps 40,000,000 acres of arid lands in Montana. The Dakota Congressmen say they will stand by the old man who holds the purse. I would like to be so instructed by this Convention. California is a country owned absolutely by railroads. Every business man who goes there must admit it. That influence controlled the Salt Lake Convention. I ask Mr. Clark and Mr. Gregory if they can deny it. There is to-day, I dislike to say it, a judge on the Supreme Bench who is actually a lobbyist in getting judges named. This I understand from my colleagues who are lawyers, and to whom is referred the recommending of judges. I refer to Judge Field, who is apparently going out of his way in these matters. I dislike to mention those things, but you should have facts. Who are the men standing by the Salt Lake proposition? Men living on the plains? No, sir; the prime movers are from small mining counties. I have said enough, gentlemen, but I am ready to answer any questions, if you desire it. If these lands are ceded to us, that will be an end to our appropriations. After having had forty or fifty millions of acres of land given to us, we will be asked to stand aside. How is the situation? Wyoming has about two-thirds of her lands surveyed; she has had Union Pacific influence. The Northern Pacific does not care about having the lands surveyed. We have hardly one-fifth surveyed in Montana. These are facts, and we want to consider them and act immediately. I would ask that some of the members who were at the Salt Lake Convention be heard from.

Mr. Carney, of Madison: Senator, what are the chances for appropriations by Congress for irrigation?

Senator Power: If we all work together, I believe we will succeed in securing such measures. When I say that, I mean we, the Representatives in Congress of the sixteen or seventeen States and Territories, comprising what is known as the arid region.

Mr. Strevell, of Custer: I suppose the ordinary parliamentary usage would be for the adoption of the resolution taken up first.

The Chairman: I think as a committee of the whole we can take no action. We can recommend to the Convention that it adopt the section.

R. H. Howey, of Lewis and Clarke: After discussion it will be proper to move a recommendation.

Mr. Strevell: I now offer as a substitute for Resolution No. 1 the following:

Resolved, That in the judgment of this Convention it is the duty of the general government to aid in the development by irrigation of the arid lands in the several states and territories where such lands exist; and while we do not deem it desirable that the control and title to such lands should pass from the general government to the several states containing them, we do nevertheless urge that at least the proceeds arising from the sale of such lands shall be applied to the supply of water for their development for the purposes of agriculture, and we urge upon our Senators and Representatives in Congress to use every effort to accomplish such legislation as will bring about this desirable result, not only in our state, but for all other states and territories similarly situated.

Mr. Strevell then addressed the Convention upon the substitute as follows:

Mr. Chairman and Gentlemen of the Convention:

Upon this substitute which I have offered it is desirable that we shall reach such a result as will be satisfactory to all. If there is any scheme or any trap I do not suppose we will fall into it. As to the first proposition I do not desire, and I shall be very brief, to be understood at any stage of this Convention as antagonizing the proposition that it is the duty of the general government to aid in the development of the arid lands in this State, because it is the duty of the general government to aid. I am going to assume that farming is the basis of this country. [Applause.] We cannot live without the productions of the farm. To invite a man to farm without water in this Western country is but little short of inviting him to a hospitable grave. Hence it becomes necessary that some other means should be devised than formerly prevailed to aid in development. That is the reason for the presence of these delegates here, because there is a condition of things here that has not been confronted before in the history of this country. It is the duty of this government to aid in the development of these arid regions. That's a proposition I am prepared to stand by in all the stages of it. In the early days of Illinois that vast domain lay there, which is now an empire, with not a railroad. Stephen A. Douglass in 1849, I think, introduced into Congress, which was passed, a bill which gave to the company which should build from one end of the state to the other every alternate section of land. Immediately, as if by magic, the state jumped to the front and is now third in the Union. So, by government aid, was the continent spanned. It is, and should be, the prime consideration of this Convention that the government shall help and assist in the development of these arid lands. Is it desirable, as the Salt Lake Convention said, to transfer the control and title of these lands to the various states? I think not [loud applause], and in a word I will tell you why. Some of you gentlemen are perfectly plain, as I am. You may protest against it when the corporations come to take those lands; your voices may be raised against it, but it will be as the breath to the idle wind. It will be accomplished, and it is our duty not to put these lands into that condition.

It is the duty of the government to provide a homestead for every poor man who wants it, and if he must have water to develop it, it is the duty of the government to aid him in that also. [Applause.] The ceding of the arid lands to the State would make necessary the establishment of tribunals to determine land contests just as it is now done by the general government. The State cannot stand the expense. For these reasons and many others I do not assent to the proposition urged by the Salt Lake Convention.

It is our duty to harmonize all the elements of this arid region just as far as we can. I would not for one moment oppose anything done by the Salt Lake Convention, because it is the duty of all so far as possible to stand together, but I cannot acquiesce in the proposition that the State should have the control and title of these arid lands. For that reason I have offered the substitute.

In conclusion I wish to say that the arid lands, undesirable as they now appear to the eye, will some day constitute the grandest portion of the whole United States. No man knows what these uniting prairies will become when the fertility which resides in their bosom is called forth by the application of water. Let us keep these questions close to the people. Keep their water, the management of it, in their hands. Under the Salt Lake resolution it can never be done.

The Chairman: As the Senator from this State has requested to hear from some of the delegates who were present at the Salt Lake Convention, I believe it would be proper for the Chairman of the Committee on Resolutions, who was in that Convention, to address the meeting.

W. A. Clark, of Silver Bow, the gentleman referred to, then addressed the Convention as follows:

Mr. President and Gentlemen:

We appear here at the call of the Governor to take into consideration a question that vitally concerns the prosperity of the State—the question of irrigation and the reclamation of the arid lands. This is in consequence of an agitation of the subject recently inaugurated in Nebraska, where a Convention was held in February last, and in which a resolution was adopted providing for a western inter-state congress to consider the question of irrigation more widely, and Salt Lake City was the place designated for the meeting. The congress was called by Governor Thomas, of Utah, in September. All the States and Territories, except two or three, which are embraced in what is termed the arid region, that great expanse of country which lies west of the 100th meridian of longitude, were there represented. The convention was composed of about five hundred delegates and remained in session three days. Many resolutions were considered, and after full and free discussion those cited in the published call of our Governor were adopted almost without dissent.

The first one involves the most important question, that of the cession by the general government to the several States and Territories of all the arid lands lying within their boundaries; and this resolution expresses the crystalized sentiment of that convention.

It was an assemblage of representative men, in the main agriculturists, but drawn from every occupation and profession, and I believe they were thoroughly identified with the industries of their respective States, and mindful of their best interests. I have no doubt that in point of intelligence and honesty of purpose they would average very well with the distinguished gentleman who has just preceded me and who so indelicately raised the question of self-interest and possibly fraud as the governing motives in that convention. It is an unjust reflection on the character of the men who were there, and, speaking for my colleagues who shared the honor with me of representing Montana on that occasion, I resent the insinuation that they were dupes, led into a trap by the representatives of railroad companies, as suggested by the gentlemen from Choteau, or participants in a movement which was prompted by incentives of fraud.

It is gratifying to find here in this body representative men from every part of the State, and that all of the principal occupations, trades and professions are represented. You have come here voluntarily to discuss a great question that concerns every inhabitant of the State, and I consider the insinuation of the gentleman who preceded me an undue reflection upon those delegates here engaged in pursuits other than agriculture. It would seem from that gentleman's remarks that we of the mining counties have no business here. He appeals to the people "from the plains" to "keep their eye on their guns," and warns them of lurking designs and dangers that threaten them. Now I venture to suggest that the people in the mining districts—and they certainly have done their part to build up the State—have its interests just as dearly at heart as have the farmers, or even the eminent gentleman himself. What concerns the welfare of one locality concerns all. We all have a right to avail ourselves of the privileges of the land laws, and all likewise of the benefits of the mineral laws.

It is a public question that we have met to discuss. Let it be free to all. I have too much confidence in the intelligence, the integrity and the magnanimity of the people of Montana, whatever may be their avocation, to believe that, in considering questions of this character, they could be largely influenced by narrow or sordid considerations.

The question before us is one of the most important that could possibly engage our attention. The mining development in this State has attained gigantic proportions. By the concentration of the highest skill and large capital, we have reached a position unparalleled in all the world. We should not permit our other great resources to lie dormant or to languish.

The importance of irrigation becomes apparent when we realize the fact that more than one-half of the agriculture of the world is dependent upon it; that two-fifths of the arable land of the United States will not surely produce crops without its aid, and that in our own State, which is estimated to contain over twenty million acres susceptible to cultivation, irrigation is absolutely essential to successful agriculture.

The artificial watering of the earth had its origin soon after the struggle of mankind for subsistence first began. Ruins of ditches and aqueducts, as well as reservoirs, are found in Asia, Africa, and all other parts of the world. Some of them were projected upon a magnificent scale. Egypt has been called the classic ground of irrigation. The Spanish Conquerors discovered upon the eastern slopes of the Andes, aqueducts as much as five hundred miles in length and reservoirs of such stupendous character, as indicated a civilization far in advance of that possessed by the Incas, and all of such permanent construction as to survive the disintegrating forces of unnumbered ages.

The Aztecs employed irrigation to increase the productiveness of their fields centuries before the fleets of their conquerors appeared on the Gulf of Mexico. In Arizona the aborigines built ditches in the valley of the Gila more than five hundred years ago, and in several localities of that Territory have been found extensive ruins of irrigation works that were built by prehistoric races.

The gradual decay of irrigation works on the peninsula of India was followed by impoverishment of the natives and in some instances by famine. The British government about thirty years since took the matter up, and has since expended about one hundred and twenty million of dollars in irrigation improvements, and as much more in building canals, highways and railroads necessary to transport the cereals that irrigation enabled them to produce, and the result was that India, next to the United States, became the largest producer of wheat, and has become a serious competitor of this country for the European markets.

Previous to the last quarter of a century the methods of application of water were rather of a crude and unscientific nature, until the needs of the Far West invoked the aid of engineering skill and reduced it to a science, and obtained the maximum results. But much more may be accomplished by impounding waters during the flood season, by which a steady supply will be insured and larger areas watered in the dry period of the year. To Montana this means a great deal. Here exist, I believe, the greatest possibilities to be found anywhere. This State is traversed by a magnificent system of mountain ranges, pregnant with mineral wealth, and clothed with measureless forests, which are great accumulators and conservators of snow and moisture and upon whose bosoms Nature has scooped out hydrographic basins, which require simply a wall at their outlet to convert them into reservoirs ample for all requirements of storage.

The innumerable streams having here their sources which furnish the waters of two of the greatest rivers of the continent are admirably located for the best possible diversion and distribution to the arable lands.

These are known to be of the greatest fertility and will produce from forty to fifty bushels of wheat to the acre, and the other grains in proportionate abundance. Consider, moreover, their contiguity to the richest mining districts that the world has ever known, which will insure a constant and advantagous market, and it becomes apparent that our State is endowed with the elements of wealth in the highest degree. At present we depend largely on other States for produce that should be raised at home. Flour, bacon, fruits, vegetables, butter, eggs and poultry, in car-load lots, are unloaded daily at our principal railway stations, and millions of dollars are sent out annually for these articles that should go into the pockets of our own farmers. The benefits resulting would exceed the calculations of the most sanguine, and the condition of the farmer here, with a market at his own door for his annual product made certain by irrigation, would present a striking contrast to that of the western farmer who is obliged to contend with drouths, distant and fluctuating markets, long hauls, extortionate charges and the competition of cheap Asiatic labor. Now what is the status of irrigation here to-day? Almost at a standstill. The lowlands lying along and near the streams were appropriated by the early settlers and watered by small ditches of easy and comparatively inexpensive construction. Moreover this character of land is of limited area compared with the broad table lands lying higher up, and the still higher and far more extensive mesas, which are even more fertile, but all require expensive canals for their proper watering.

Individual effort has almost reached its limit and it becomes necessary to invoke the assistance of capital or depend on government or State appropriations. Hence we are confronted with the important problem as to how we can best effect the reclamation of these lands and provide homes for the people.

There are some, Mr. President, who are content to lean on the arm of the government and expect it to come to the rescue with liberal and adequate appropriations. Others despair of accomplishing anything of consequence from that quarter and believe it is better to ask that the lands be ceded to the States. This was the conclusion arrived at at Salt Lake, and the people of Montana are asked to cooperate with this plan. Mr. President, I am in accord with this theory, but I desire to hear a full discussion of the question in this Convention, and if thereafter I am convinced that my position is not wise or tenable I say to you frankly that I will abandon it. But I want to hear something reasonable and definite presented, and not mere vague assertion and inuendo as we have heard this morning.

I am convinced that the time is now opportune when the government may advantageously dispense with its land system.

About all of the available public land is now occupied. I am informed that the number of acres now unsold amounts to less than a million. The arid region is practically valueless without water, and this I do not believe the government can or will provide in a prompt or economical manner. The conditions existing in the several states are entirely different, and no uniform system that the government would necessarily have to adopt would be applicable everywhere or secure the most advantageous application of water. A law suitable to New Mexico would be impractical for the needs of Montana. Utah requires entirely different regulations from Dakota. Each state can best legislate for itself, particularly as each state has a different statute governing water rights.

Again, we of the West all know how difficult it is to procure appropriations of any considerable proportions. The states lying east of the arid belt would all oppose it, apprehending competition in the cereal markets, and being somewhat jealous of the Far West. This subject has already received some attention in Congress, but so far without practical results.

One hundred thousand dollars were appropriated in 1888, and the year following two hundred and fifty thousand dollars more, for the purpose of surveying the irrigable lands. This was a commendable movement, and I have no doubt but that much valuable data and information have been secured through government inquiry. But let us now inquire what became of that money. The whole matter was placed in the hands of Major Powell, director of the geological survey, who diverted and used up one hundred and eighty thousand dollars in making topographic surveys and maps thereof, claiming that this work was a necessary preliminary to any engineering work. The Senate Irrigation Commission, very justly, severely criticised this action as an unlawful diversion of money that they considered indefensible.

Mr. Power: Mr. Clark, I would like to correct you on the statements made by you concerning appropriations.

Mr. Clark: Very well.

Mr. Power: In the first session of the Fifty-first Congress there was appropriated for the Agricultural Bureau the sum of $889,000, and during the last session an additional sum of $812,000. Major Powell is not under the direction of the Agricultural Bureau. A great deal of the money has gone to furnish positions for Powell's friends from the South, East and North, and to his cousins and his aunts.

Mr. Clark: I do not accept the statements of the gentlemen as any correction of what I said. They refer to an entirely different subject. I said nothing about the Agricultural Bureau or appropriations therefor, but the remarks of the gentleman from Choteau are corroborative of the theory I advance touching the futility of seeking appropriations in aid of any Western enterprise, with the expectation of having the funds properly applied.

Mr. President, we are not without precedent on the subject at issue. The swamp lands were donated to the states in 1849, and so far as I can learn it was considered a wise movement, which worked out admirably. Every consideration urged in behalf of that measure would apply with equal or greater force to the cession of the arid lands. It has been suggested that this theory, if carried out, would encourage jobbery and corruption in our Legislatures, and that in the control and disposition of the lands, monopolies of land and water franchises would be created.

It is a well known fact that water is the key to the land; that the latter without the former is almost valueless, and there is the danger, under existing circumstances, to which we are now exposed.

The best water privileges in the State are now being absorbed by individuals and corporations which, while they may not improve these lands, will have a monopoly of the most desirable of them, and this will seriously handicap and complicate future operations more and more as the matter is delayed.

As to the other objection, do we not trust our Legislatures to regulate our most vital interests and make laws controlling every species of property? If we cannot trust them to control and dispose of the arid lands if donated to the State, in God's name what is to become of the great grant of school lands that were given to us with statehood? I am not one of those who believe in the total depravity of human nature. I think our interests much safer in the keeping of our Legislative Assembly than in that of Congress.

Now, I say, let the states own the lands, and they will take care of them and dispose of them judiciously, without fostering monopolies or allowing the practice of extortion. We are asked how this can be accomplished. I say, leave that problem to the future. It will be of easy solution. Canals and reservoirs may be constructed by the State, and the proceeds of the sale of the land applied to reimbursement, or a law enacted creating irrigation districts, whereby the people themselves can carry out the system of reclamation. Such a law was put into operation in 1877 in the Orange Free State of South Africa, creating a board in each district having corporate authority and the power to issue bonds by creating a first lien on all of the property of the district. This is said to work very satisfactorily. A similar law, called the Wright bill, was enacted in California in 1887, which works admirably. The State Supreme Court has repeatedly affirmed the validity of its provisions. The bonds, secured by mortgage, run twenty to thirty years, and afford a safe, permanent and desirable security, that is eagerly sought by investors in the Eastern states and of Europe. There is another question which is intimately associated with irrigation, and that is the preservation of our forests. They perform an important service in sheltering the snows and holding them until late in summer, to feed gradually the sources of the rivers, and I hold that these lands also should be ceded to the states.

I feel assured that the people of Montana would exercise more care in the protection of the timber in our forests, while at the same time providing the inhabitants with what they require in their various pursuits, and much more satisfactorily than the government can or will possibly do. Forest fires generally destoy more timber in one year than would be consumed in fifty years. As it is now, the Department of the Interior, in framing regulations governing the cutting of timber on the public domain, is influenced largely by the American Forestry Association. What do these people know about the forests of the Rocky Mountains or the needs of the people there? Scarcely anything. Perhaps few of them have ever been as far in this direction as Chicago. They call that the "Far West."

Senator Power: Would you also include the mineral lands in the proposed cession?

Mr. Clark: That is a proposition not contemplated in the resolution, and I have not fully considered it; but I would suggest that in view of the history of national legislation whereby large grants of our best lands have been made to railroad corporations by statutes so loosely drawn that we find those corporations now laying claim to millions of acres of our mineral lands, with a good prospect of success according to recent decisions, it would probably be a wise provision to include these lands also with the others. No Montana Legislature would ever frame such a law as that. I think we could depend upon it that the people and not the corporations under state legislation would possess and enjoy the mineral lands.

Senator Power: You stated that in India there had been expended more than a hundred millions of dollars in irrigation works. I would like to know how that money was raised.

Mr. Clark: The necessary funds were appropriated by the British government. The conditions here and there are entirely different. The people of India are very poor, having few resources aside from their fertile soil. Self interest dictated to the government the [expediency of these appropriations, and it was done with a lavish hand, and the results confirmed the wisdom of the enterprise. We are able to take care of ourselves, and besides we might wait a hundred years and then not obtain any government aid commensurate with the magnitude of the scheme in contemplation.

Now, Mr. President, I have concluded all that I desire to say at present upon this subject. I thank you, gentlemen, for the patient attention you have accorded me. Whatever may be the result of the discussion of this question in this Convention, I trust that the agitation of the subject will continue until some practical system is inaugurated that will mark the beginning for our young State of a new era of prosperity.

Mr. Clark's remarks were frequently greeted with applause.

H. P. Rolfe, of Cascade: I move that the speeches after this be limited to five minutes.

Mr. Word, of Lewis and Clarke: I move to amend by making it fifteen minutes. I want to say something myself.

Mr. Burton, of Choteau: I move that the motion as amended be laid on the table.

The Chairman: The motion is upon the proposition to lay the motion and amendment on the table.

Mr. Howey, of Lewis and Clarke: I move that the committee arise and ask leave to sit again.

The committee arose and on motion a recess was taken until 2 p. m.

FRIDAY AFTERNOON.

At 2 p. m. the Convention was called to order by Vice President Irvin. On motion the Convention resolved itself into a committee of the whole, with Mr. Chisholm in the chair.

Mr. Charles A. Gregory, of Gallatin County, spoke as follows:

Mr. President and Gentlemen of the Convention:

I had the honor to second the resolution offered by Judge Strevell, and I rise to speak in support of that resolution and to express my disapproval of the first section of the platform of the Salt Lake Congress.

I speak, not because I love the melody of my own voice, but because moved by a sincere conviction, and appreciating the great importance of the question at issue. I feel I have a message to convey to this Convention out of the depths of my heart, and out of a judgment made up upon reflection.

No speaker can magnify beyond its just merits the importance of the question involved in the needs and demands of the arid region;

it is the most important question before the American Congress to-day; it involves money value surpassing all other money values that Congress deals with put together; it involves the exercises of all the brain power in statesmanship that the Nation can command, to work out the details of the questions which now press and which will arise in the future in legislation and in the application of scientific methods to conserve waters, to prevent floods, to preserve forests, to build reservoirs, to mark out irrigation districts, to compose interstate complications and international difficulties.

Reference has been made on this floor to the origin of this demand to cede the public domain to the states wherein situate, and to the conduct of the Utah Congress. It is thought the Utah Congress has given out a manufactured opinion, and that the Congress was under such control as to make it a foregone conclusion that it would pass a resolution asking the United States Congress to cede the public lands to the States.

In reading the report of the proceedings of that Congress, we are struck with names and situation of the persons who appear to have been the leaders in the debate. We naturally ask, who owns these men, or what do these men own? One of the gentlemen was introduced as the General Land Agent of the Central and Southern Pacific Railroad Companies, and was also known as land commissioner of the Oregon & California, and of the Houston & Texas Railroad Companies. These are surely positions of honor and trust. Another of the gentlemen was known as a very extensive owner of lands in the arid region and to be engaged in irrigation development in Nevada to an extent that astonishes men of the ordinary business abilities. Such is perceived to be the situation of two men who with great address and with mental ability equal to their boldness and address, dominated in influence in that convention. Another was so circumstanced as to lead to the supposition that personal ambitions and property interests and hope of opportunities might govern to a large extent the position he took on this question of State control of public lands.

One of these gentlemen, indeed, said in that congress, "there is no room for modesty in this bustling and active world of ours;" and whether that be a fact or not, he clearly showed that he did not occupy "that room."

I recall that some of the Utah orators boasted they would carry their plan by the force of the impact. I quote their words. But the gravity of the good sense of the people is now aroused and set in motion against the Utah plan. We shall not find it overcome by the "impact" of the Utah demand, and the future "impact" of the blows will be less and less felt. The people have been thinking meanwhile. The speculators and the cattlemen who want to get hold of great ranges as a private property, through the channel of State ownership, now perceive that the farmers must be consulted in this movement. You, farmers, are here to-day; what do you say?

The Utah platform has been endorsed by some other conventions. The proceedings of these several irrigation conventions which have preceded this one, and in which the movers have succeeded in getting a vote for the Utah first plank, remind me of the experiments in natural philosophy and in magic, where a small mass of matter overcomes and regulates a much larger, if there but be an anticipation of motion by the velocity of one before the other is prepared to act or to resist. As the explosive power of a little gunpowder will overcome gravity because the latter is slower in resisting the motion of the mass.

I do not wish to deal in personalities, and if I may be permitted to criticise somewhat in the tone of censure any of the remarks of those who have preceded me, I should say that the argument drawn from the situation and relations of the persons or the motives found on the other side of this question, is not the best argument to use. So that the honorable Senator who has spoken on this subject, while he may be right in his conclusions, has not sufficiently stated the grounds of his conclusions. However, it is always pertinent to learn all that can be learned of the motives and environments of the men who originated the segregation plan.

A novel plan is proposed. Who proposes it, and who are for it? The answer to these questions will create in men's minds, naturally enough, a predisposition to reject or favor the plan, according as we may perceive that the plan runs along in harmony with the selfish side of their business, attended with grave danger to public interests, or that the plan is evidently good for the public. The force of the argument is not toward the decision of the question on its merits, but it is used as a caution that we be not led to adopt the conclusion merely because able and ingenius men have recommended it to us. The moral force of the majority vote at the Utah Congress is broken in view of certain facts of the nature I have just mentioned, and further in view of the fact that there were able men in that Congress who did not vote for the ceding of the lands to the states, and who pointed out strong objections and dangers arising out of such a plan of dealing with the public domain. Another consideration that will weaken the moral effect of a majority vote in that Congress is that it was called to petition Congress to cede the lands to the states. Men were designated to go to that Congress, naturally enough, who favored the object of the call. Its opponents would not be solicited. Hence, so far as this Convention here assembled to-day is concerned, this question need not be seriously prejudiced in favor of the State control of the lands by the action of the Utah Congress. And to descend to lesser matters, nor need it be prejudiced by the fact of arrangement to have as the President of this Convention one who is in favor of the Utah plan, and to have the Chairman of the Committee of the Whole in favor of such plan, and to have the orator who was to speak first in this Convention one who went to school to the Utah Congress, and to have to him accorded the floor for a good hour. Since these things are so, and, as may be claimed, are so in their favor by accident, I did regret that any one could be found who, upon the close of that speech of the gentleman thus put forward, should arise from their side of the question and move to limit the rest of the debate to five-minute speeches. We have come hither on business of State from distant places at expense of time and money, and we are here as a deliberative assembly, concerned to consider with circumspection and reflection the most important measure before the American people; and yet some delegate thinks he aids the cause of truth and right by shutting the mouths of those who do not agree with his views. Such a course I deem an insult to the intelligence and fairmindedness of this Convention.

Emboldened by your evident interest in the question and your eager looks of inquiry for some statement of grounds of rejection of this Utah plan, I shall not trouble myself to look at the hour glass while speaking, and, though I shall be brief, I will be limited only by the necessity of the statement and your continued approval. I speak under a duty.

If it should be known that I am the farmer's friend, that I am the advocate for the protection of the rights of the working classes, and the friend of every humble citizen throughout the United States who has rights in the public domain, and that I stand against monopoly, I should think this the proudest distinction that could be bestowed upon me.

Here is a question of changing by the wholesale, and at once, in one broad legislative action, the tenure and ownership and mode of disposition of a vast domain, equal in extent to something like two-fifths of the United States, outside of Alaska, lessened by the amount of lands already reduced to private ownership. It is a question also of changing the national policy which has existed for a century, and in later days has been improved upon by its mineral, timber, homestead and desert entry laws, which has grown into a vast administrative system, and which has hitherto worked to well as to challenge the praise and admiration of wise and patriotic statesmen. New physical conditions presented in the arid region require some modification of this system. Under the existing system of public domain policy there have been usefully distributed seven hundred millions of acres of lands; there have been usefully expended under that policy more than two hundred and twenty-three millions of dollars. There has thus grown in practice a great departmental administration under the Secretary of the Interior, which, resting at the capital of a great nation, surveys, investigates and executes over a field that covers many states and territorial regions, many differences of climate, a variety of land, mineral, agricultural, pastoral and timber, and the so-called waste lands, and which in a measure affects and controls climatic conditions in and over vast regions of land surface.

Your deliberations, then, will be clothed with dignity and importance, by reason of the importance of the issues which your resolutions shall tend to affect and mould. A weight of responsibility should press on your minds equal to the gravity of the questions involved. The gravity of such questions will be more clearly apprehended if we stop to consider in whose interests you are about to act. Is it a matter that pertains to one state alone? Aye, even to one nation alone? Is it for a present and temporary interest you are to deliberate? Is it alone the welfare of the existing generation that shall concern you? Are not all the arid states and territories interested? are not all the states of the Union interested? Is not the coming generation to be affected by the tendency of your recommendations? Are not future generations upon their coming to feel the impress of this day's work at your hands? I would not miss, then, the opportunity to strengthen and deepen this feeling of responsibility to local and to general interests and to the immediate and to future time? Let us dwell on it for a while at least, and then, when our mood is fitted to form a conclusion, let us conclude and resolve in the face of all these stupendous interests with what of unselfishness and with what of wisdom we may.

The act of sitting in this Convention and voting for a string of resolutions might seem slight and inconsequential, unless we halt for a moment. Our heads are full of our own individual affairs. Men walk in accustomed paths often without heeding the ground they are passing over till they come face to face with some new object to arrest their attention. Here, before us, are objects and subjects that should startle us to a halt, and hold us to rest for calm thought.

Let us lead our minds in our deliberations in this Convention step by step to the things we are contemplating in this wrench to our land system. First, to what end was the system framed? And is that a good end or final purpose, and will a change lead to better results? Having considered the end or final purpose of our present system, let us ask if the means of attaining such end are better furnished by the several states and territories separately than by the united action of the nation. Great expenditure of money is involved in this action, and in the details to a useful result. Will feeble and poor states and territories be able to spend millions on millions of dollars in separately caring for these great interests?

Bear in mind that if you take by grant from the nation all this great domain of arid lands you take upon yourselves the mighty and oppressive burden of reclamation at your own expense, unaided by national appropriation.

One great harm to grow out of ceding the lands to the states is that the lands will be sold out in job lots and get into the hands of schemers and monopolists. They will not be sacredly kept for the occupancy and ownership of the people and the poor man. The declaimers for the ceding plan tell us, with an air of surprise and with pity for our fears, that this is not possible; that we must not distrust the ability of a free people in a free country and under Democratic rule to protect themselves; that we thus slander the people and insult the legislatures; that we asperse the integrity and honesty of the people. This reply sounds well and it is expected to put us to the blush. We know that experience teaches us we are right to take counsel of our fears. Some of the states have given us examples of warning. I cannot stay on this for instances of proof. Public men know them well enough. But the people know these things. There is a popular distrust of state legislatures which may be said to characterize a large portion of the American people at the present time.

The details of the Constitutions of the four most recently formed States, lying all of them in the arid region, illustrate this fixed tendency in American politics—they frame their constitutions to declare what the respective State legislatures cannot be permitted to do.

The principal prohibitions on the legislatures are: On enacting any private or special legislation; on extinguishing or releasing the obligations of corporations or of individuals to the State; on legislative bribery; on personal or private interest in a bill in any member; on irregular form in framing bills; on appropriations of moneys; on performing legislative functions by deputy; on loaning the credit of the State to corporations; on authorizing lotteries; and on entertaining money bills during the last hours of the legislature.

These new constitutions suggest that the people have lost confidence in their State legislatures, and thus the people have sought to anticipate great evils by limiting powers of the legislature; by telling them what they may do and what they may not do.

This is the undeniable answer to the declamation of orators who boast the integrity of legislatures. It is known that many honest legislators are brought and weedled to do the things by intriguing members and lobbyists, which in the innocence of the well intentioned members they never knew the iniquity of till the wrong is consummated.

These considerations convince one that "the people" will be set against the ceding of lands to the full control of the States. We do not distrust the ability of "the people" to take care of their own interests. When they are assembled in conventions they do that very well. The result of this Convention will show their sagacity. It is only that the people distrust the influences that may be brought to bear on their agents.

I tell the politicians who hold the strings of this kite which they are now flying before the face of the people, that they will ere long bring down the lightning on themselves. This Utah plan is not to be a popular plan. The people will continue to regard the national domain as their heritage—to be kept sacredly for the benefit of the poor man, the homeseeker and the settler, throughout the United States.

It is a bad thing for a State to own large properties of this nature. Such political institutions as States are not made for monetary corporations, or corporations to deal in property; they are framed to preserve order, to punish crimes, to protect property rights, to protect the weak against the strong, and there the proper functions cease. The people know this and will not wish to have new temptations to fraud and to monopoly set on foot, as would be done by the Utah plan.

The Salt Lake City Congress did resolve that its members, as a majority, were in favor of granting in trust, upon such conditions as may serve the public interest, to the States and Territories needful of irrigation, all lands now a part of the public domain within such States and Territories, excepting mineral lands, for the purpose of developing irrigation, to render the lands now arid fertile and capable of supporting a population.

This Convention, under the call of Governor Toole of Montana, is called, it is declared in the call, because it is "deemed advisable to obtain a direct expression of the people of Montana upon the resolutions adopted by the Salt Lake City congress."

This is a useful purpose. One will hardly think, however, that a convention made up by the selection of a few delegates by the boards of county commissioners will necessarily reflect the wishes or views of the people on this topic It would seem more to the purpose to declare that a convention should be held to take under consideration the matters referred to in the resolution of the Utah congress, to the end that the people of the State may hear arguments for and against the recommendations embraced in the Utah platform. The discussion of the questions involved would be highly useful and instructive. Such discussion would prepare the public to make up its mind on these resolutions.

I have somewhere else said the Convention was supposed to be called "to foster interest in the question of ceding public lands to the States in the arid region." It is charged, and it is thought, that there is a desire on the part of some interested cliques to create a public opinion in favor of such a course. This is not illegitimate work, unless the open and full opportunity to express the opposite opinion is denied to the people. That opportunity must come, however, and the forum for its discussion is the halls of Congress. The participators in that discussion will be the members of Congress from all parts of the United States. I shall assume members of Congress from the parts east of the 100th meridian of west longitude can intelligently study and consider this question; as can also members from the arid regions. Such intelligent study of the question may bring wiser results of legislation than if the solution of the question is left to rest on the demands of voluntary conventions not made up of delegates chosen by the people. The choice of members of Congress from the States may yet turn on this single issue; and when it shall so turn, then we may believe that the mind of the people will be ascertained. In the meantime agitation, discussion and instruction is what may be best sought after. Keep these conventions going. The uses of these conventions are the agitation of the question and the instruction to grow out of them. We all profess to want the same thing, i. e., what may best serve the public interest. My insistance will be that the whole of the vast interests involved shall be duly considered, that the views of men who have been prepared by study and observation and familiarity with the subjects, may be brought out; and that we may respectfully hear their conclusions. Against the quickly pronounced resolves of delegates chosen to declare their own views, and who do not profess special preparation of mind to form such views, I would wish the people to weigh the views of men who do possess special preparation of mind on these questions. I would call an architect to advise me on the plan and construction of an important edifice; I would advise with a lawyer rather than a tinsmith, to guide me as to my contract rights and liabilities, and equally wise would it be to consult scientific men and statesmen on grave questions of preservation of natural streams of water, reservoirs of water and head waters, and forest regions, and as to legislation for the best public interest, and long enduring public interest. Trained and able men are in the employment of the government. Let us have their advice. I cannot think that separate States can deal with an international question of right to use and conserve natural waters, or that they can deal with interstate questions of the same nature, or that poor and feeble States can sustain the pecuniary burdens of scientific investigation and publication for instruction, of geological and geographical surveys, nor of building reservoirs and canals. Or is it supposed that Congress will wisely cede all these lands to the States and still continue all its expenditures in their preparation for sale and disposal the same as though it were still charged with holding such lands in trust for all the citizens of the nation?

It is now certain that these matters will be carried on at national expense; if the new plan is adopted, it will no longer at least be certain that we should have that aid. It is probable we should lose such aid.

f I have dwelt somewhat at length on the Utah congress it is because in the call for this Convention in which we are speaking the Governor has said that the purpose of calling the Convention is to take the sense of the citizens of this State on the matters resolved on by the Utah congress. The Utah congress is made the leader to form opinion in favor of its plan. I shall venture to predict that your voice will call a halt in this movement, and make a recommendation to Congress that shall fix the attention of Congressmen from the east and from the south, on our needs, while showing we do not ask what is injurious.

Now we have been presented with the substance of the argument in favor of the Utah plan, by one who is selected as its exponent because of his ability to set forth the argument, and because he did attend that congress, and having been fully instructed, crammed down to the bottom and filled full to the top with the utmost argument presented in that congress by the most able and skillful attorneys for a certain faction, he brings here to us that argument. Necessarily I can comment on that argument. I listened to his speech with profound respect, and with the utmost interest, in order to discover the reasons for the Utah plan, and to give to him the benefit of every good reason he could assign.

I desire to ask you if am not right in the inference from his speech that his argument is this: We want the arid domain placed within control of the States respectively in which it is situate, for two reasons. One is that we need development of irrigation, and in this matter Congress will not help us. Secondly, that seventeen States individually, chopping this arid domain into seventeen fractions, can better manage these seventeen fractions than the United States Congress can manage the national domain as an entirety.

I grant you we want irrigation development (letting this phrase cover the whole subject). We want this and we want it as rapidly as it may be done, because we want to give to all who seek it the benefit of cheap land and great crops in this region which we know is suited to be the habitation of the highest civilization of the human family. I do not admit that Congress will not help us. That, at least from the stand of those who state it to be so, is an unimproved proposition. I do not believe it. It may be contradicted from our present knowledge of legislation. None of us expect, or, I may say, desire that the nation should build irrigating canals, but to preserve forests, to make reservoirs, promote surveys and make laws to bring the land and water into close relation, and to aid in some manner the irrigation development, is expected and desired. Appropriations to this end have been made already; we want them continued or increased. Already a standing committee has been made in the United States Senate on irrigation; already a committee is formed in the House on this subject. A bureau of irrigation inquiry is established. We want it more amply provided for. The mind of the people is being aroused to all these matters, to their importance, and to our needs. Therefore I deny that Congress will not aid in this matter. I can conceive, too, that the impatience of young and sparsely peopled States, and the eager haste of speculators in lands and canals will not be pleased with any slowness on the part of Congress; but I can also conceive that too great haste can be made and bold expenditures entered on in advance of the means of a population to justify or to sustain them.

The next point is: It is claimed the several states will better manage the lands and make better money provision than Congress could do. This is certainly not so in my judgment. A nation of sixty-five millions of people, possessing more natural resources of wealth and taxable ability than any other nation on the globe, is surely better able to sustain the burden of providing money for the aid of this kind of improvement than a few feeble and poor states. If states should undertake any works of this nature as states, they would not do any great things, or, entering upon great things, they would become bankrupt. But I do not believe in states doing any of these things. If states do not make the improvements, then individuals, or private corporations, or municipal corporations in the form of irrigation districts will do it, and in either of these events they will be better done while the domain is controlled by the nation and under its laws than if the same were granted to the several states.

It is not for me to work out the details of any plan. I am only to show that change of ownership and control of the public lands will not help matters; or rather I should say, the burden is on those who would force a change to show that it is free from dangers and is beneficial. We who are conservative stand upon the ancient ways. If any would advise to make a change, let them prove that such a change is clearly for the best interests of the people. This they have not done. Has the policy recommended in the Utah resolution ever been fully considered, or, as some may ask, ever been honestly put before the people?

Most of the voters of the United States, we may feel sure, have never thought of it. Few of the members of Congress have ever considered it. It is new to them, and I believe those who have heard of the demand for this action, outside of interested parties, have not thought of it as a likely or as a desirable measure.

The recommendation is indeed coupled with the condition that the "trust be upon such conditions as may serve the public interest."

The trust is now already in such hands, and upon such conditions as may best serve the public interest. It may in its present hands be moulded. It is a plastic trust, shapeable to the best needs of each state and of the whole of the people of the United States

The petition to the United States Congress to convey the lands to the State in trust is but a term or phrase to allure, since I notice that in the arguments at the Utah Congress as reported the position is insisted on that the title to the lands shall pass absolutely to the State, to do with such lands as they please, the trust, so called, being simply that the proceeds of such lands shall be used for furthering irrigation, or for irrigation and for school purposes.

"The trust to be upon such conditions as may serve the public interest." Here is the rub. You who demand a ceding of these lands to the State say, among other reasons, that the present law under which citizens may acquire lands is not well adapted to the conditions that obtain in the arid region. Such a thing as changes and amendments is known to the law makers. Remove this imperfection then.

If the ownership and control of the public domain passes from the nation to the several states, the land surveys, special examinations, explorations, educational publications at national expense naturally cease. To continue them separated from the trust is to keep things together that are incongruous. To sell my farm to another man and then for the grantee to expect me to survey his lines and run his ditches and fence and break up his land is not in harmony with our ideas of obligation and duty. How are seventeen states and territories to carry on the great measures, which cost millions of dollars annually, that we are now agreed are useful and necessary in preparing the lands for occupation? The speaker who preceded me is not fortunate in his allusion to state control of lands. Texas and California are melancholy illustrations of the improvidence of guardianship of public lands.

If the states obtain control of all the lands, except mineral, imagine what opportunities for corrupt lobbying would be opened in seventeen different capitals. A pandemonium and a riot of corruption will ensue. Arizona has a population by the census of 1890 of 59,601. How many able and intrigueing men in that state will it take to cut off every homestead right in the future, every desert entry right, timber and mineral claim in many instances? And how long will it be before a few rich land barons will be the owners of most of the 80,000,000 acres of lands there? California is a state where individuals have big holdings. These big grants and big acquisitions of lands are recognized as a blight on the prosperity of the State; they are also an injustice to the rest of the citizens not sinister enough or not dexterous enough to get these big possessions. But these things are not to be encouraged by any forms of law or by any policy of public management.

Said Mr. Estee, of California, in that Utah Congress: "I know one man who owns 258,000 acres of valley land in California, and every foot of that 258,000 acres is in one of the richest valleys of that great State, and there is not an acre of it that is either mountain or hill land."

I read in a government document, House of Representatives, United States Congress, report of Select Committee on Irrigation, February 11, 1891, that one firm of partners owns in California the water, or controls the water, that will irrigate 2,000,000 acres of land; and they now control 350,000 to 400,000 acres. This is an unjust agrandizement. These great possessions are irresistably inviting to an agrarian experiment. These are topics for communism to harp on. Hateful as this state of things is, it is not an animadversion on the men who own these properties that I make. I point the moral to another purpose. It is unjust that the system of government policy should have made this thing possible. Avoid it then as soon as possible and as strenuously as possible in your future policy. A pestilence is not so much to be dreaded. Think you a poor man from Missouri can move then to Arizona and get land and water at a cheap rate? Can a farmer go thither then from Holland and get his farm on any terms except as speculators may dictate?

I name Arizona as an instance. Will it be any better than in Nevada, in New Mexico, in Idaho, or Montana, or Wyoming or other states? Montana is of course virtuous. We have seen no party strife there; no attempt to steal government control there. Does any junto of able schemers like these opportunities? Do they covet them? And will the proposed measure make the opportunity, and then make it easy to seize all the advantages of such opportunities? The instinct of the average citizen tells him that this is the probable outcome of such a measure of cession as is proposed. This argument against the measure is felt to be a weighty one, and is answered by saying that the virtue of the governing bodies of the several States will keep watch and ward over the interests of the poor man! I think I would not tempt this boasted virtue so far and so needlessly. You say Congress will do nothing further for you. How do you know? Appeal to Congress for suitable and reasonable aid.

Take your map of the arid west and see where all the interstate waters are located. You will find all of the Missouri headwaters lie in the Rocky Mountains, and within the states of Colorado, Wyoming and Montana. You will be able to find all the Columbia's headwaters heading in Montana and Wyoming. Study the source and course of the Snake River. You may find the Rio Grande heading in Colorado. You trace the Wind, Bear and Green Rivers, the Grand, the Gunnison and San Juan, to their fountains and run them down to their mouth. Some of them tributary and headwater supplies of the Colorado River, and all of them heading in Wyoming and Colorado. Search elsewhere and you will find no interstate headwaters of any large value. Lake Tahoe, in California and Nevada may not be omitted; its importance entitles it to a reference. These three states, Colorado, Wyoming and Montana, each of them declare all natural waters to belong to the state. Hence they control all the valuable stream waters at their sources. Who shall umpire the interstate disputes when water grows more valuable and more scarce to the cultivated land area than now? You say the nation and its tribunals, perhaps. Truly. Then why seek to destroy the jurisdiction in rem, the power over the thing itself, which is the most salutory feature of our present system.

I may not omit to mention that British Columbia and Old Mexico have a finger in the pie. Is it a salutary thing to so place states in antagonism to these fringing notions as to stir up strife? But you say the strife is begun. Mexico frets, her right hand lifted; and British Columbia is on her guard, in the attitude of parry. Well, then, keep the matter where it will be no worse, and where it may, by prudence and forbearance and wisdom and unity, become much better.

I will not point to where, nor with what interest, nor in what selfishness this movement began. That would excite prejudice against it, and what I wish is candor, examination and reflection. If the policy is wise, no matter who pushes it forward, nor where it started.

Is the proposed change an improvement? Merely because it is a change, is it good? I do not hesitate to state my views. It is the cautionary signal held up by one humble citizen while the train is still getting under way, and while it is easy to slack up.

Congress had best administer in the public domain everywhere. The poor man is thus better off all over the states. The subject matter in all its details is then under a control that will enforce uniformity in the care and disposal of parcels of the public domain, and thus only can this be done. The nation of 65,000,000 of people can bear the burden of expense incidental to such control better than states poor in means of raising money and spare in populations, and new means and avenues of legislative corruption are thus kept from being opened up.

Many persons will stigmatize this demand for ceding lands as the biggest scheme for personal aggrandizement ever broached before the American people.

Congress will not fail in due time to meet all the just demands of the irrigation districts. Bills are now before Congress on this subject of great importance. Some worthy, some crude, perhaps, but these are attempts in the right direction.

A wise Congress will not fail to keep in perpetuity the heads of all the principal streams and forest and water reservations. The pastoral or water-gathering lands above 5,000 feet in altitude should be retained and only parted with where it is known that no impediment is thus created in the gathering and flow of waters. The value of the arid lands is in the waters.

My watchword is "extension of irrigation under national control" (not at national expense), gradual, sure, and up to the point to meet the wants of the coming millions of people into the arid region. Twenty years from now 100,000,000 of people will dwell in these United States, and the abundance of agricultural wealth to come out of the arid region by means of irrigation will be known and appreciated then as it is not now.

May the deliberations of this Convention be of use to all the people of all the states.

Mr. Carney, of Madison: There are quite a number of us old farmers here who have listened very attentively to quite a number of eloquent speeches. We are not familiar, however, with oratory as we are with practical farming. Therefore we would like to ask a few questions in order that some eloquent gentleman might throw some light on the subject. Thus far they have failed to do so. Show us the man who is going to be benefited by the State getting the land. What is going to become of the poor man's homestead rights? The man who starts out without money, how is he going to get hold of it if the State secures it? We can look back upon the history of the farmers for the past few years. Some of them are making money out of the soil, and I venture to say that there are large numbers of the farmers of Montana that have fallen short of making both ends meet within the last three years. I am simply asking these questions for ourselves. We are not orators or talkers. We can think and theorize and read perhaps as well as some that can do more talking. I believe you will find that the agricultural people will bring a majority against it.

Mr. A. C. Botkin: The fifteen-minute rule can be divided by three. The argument ad hominum has been introduced not by those who favor the expression contained in the Salt Lake platform. You have heard certain things from the lips of Senator Power and Mr. Gregory, charging that the Salt Lake Convention was under the personal influence of railroad men. These are the gentlemen who are held before us as a warning, as reasons why we should not support the expression of the Salt Lake platform. Now, the argument ad hominum having been introduced by the gentleman, let us pursue it into the other part. Whom do we find on this floor who are the most active and efficient in opposing the Salt Lake platform? I will name Mr. Z. T. Burton, Charles A. Gregory and Mr. Thompson and others that I might mention who are connected with irrigation enterprises in this State. I feel myself highly honored to be here with these gentlemen who are engaged in an effort to solve this problem of irrigation. The ownership of the water involves the control of the sale, the ability of the owner of the water to fix rates, and involves a taxation power more dangerous than anything that we repose in our representatives in our Legislative Assembly. Let us guard against that and against the growth of these great water barons.

In criticising Mr. Strevell's substitute the latter gentleman asked if Mr. Botkin knew that from the sales of government land the State had already received $20,000 since its admission into the Union.

Mr. Donald Bradford: I would like to correct. The lands were sold over in the City of Missoula. They were town lots.

Mr. R. O. Hickman: The State received $18,707.04, being five per cent. of the land sales. Missoula is a different matter altogether.

Mr. Botkin: According to Judge Strevell's substitute, irrigation works are to be constructed from the proceeds of the sales of lands which cannot be sold until after the works are constructed. In speaking of the Salt Lake Convention, Mr. Botkin said he had been one of the delegates, and did not believe he had fallen into any trap.

B. F. Shuart, of Yellowstone, then addressed the Convention as follows:

Mr. President and Gentlemen of the Convention:

I did not have the pleasure of being a member of the Salt Lake Convention. I have read its proceedings. The first resolution now under discussion is based upon three assumptions. The first is that in the development of the arid region we have reached a crisis. It is said about all has been accomplished that can be accomplished by individual enterprise. There is force in that statement The second assertion is that the general government cannot be depended upon for the reclamation of these lands. I feel there is great force in that statement, these arid empires of the area of the United States. The magnitude of this undertaking in Montana is something wonderful. I find from my reading of engineers' reports that a very conservative estimate is that the lands can be reclaimed at $6 per acre. If we have here in Montana 18,500,000 acres of arable lands that it will cost $6 per acre to reclaim, we are confronted at once with a cost of $110,-000,000. Is there any one here who supposes for one moment that that there is any use to even look to the general government for appropriations, going into the subject of figures, in reclaiming these lands? I think it is useless, to say nothing of fifteen states or territories. So we can see that there is a great deal to say on this subject. Still there is another assumption. That is, inasmuch as the general government cannot be relied on, the general government ought to cede the lands to the State; then the problem is solved. That is an untrue proposition, and I am very sorry that there are any personal reflections in this matter. There are reasons which underlie those Salt Lake resolutions. The first objection to that resolution is this, that it is in the interest of the monopolists. The theory given is that reclamation should be tried. You know it is the time honored policy of our government to distribute public lands in small holdings to the actual settler. It is recognized that the home is one of the vital factors in upbuilding a commonwealth, and it is this principle which the government recognizes in dispensing these lands to multiply the homes. So it has ever been the disposition to distribute the domain in small holdings to actual settlers. And any policy which tends to destroy that principle tends to destroy the heritage of the common people. The difficulties in the way of the State undertaking the reclamation of these lands have been very ably stated. Our State Constitution limits the indebtedness to $3,000,000, and $2,500,000 are now consumed in the running expenses of the State. Should these lands be ceded it would require, as I have shown, over $100,000,000 for their reclamation, to say nothing of the amount to take care of them. In some of the states where lands have been ceded in limited quantities the corporations have been allowed to reclaim them. This is done in Colorado, where the state sells the lands to corporations, and allowing them to reclaim and sell to actual settlers. Now, then, it is just so in California. You have heard the plan which is pursued there. Do you know what it means to have these lands reclaimed in that state? We find by examination that the farmers are required all over this arid region to pay from $5 to $8. After they are reclaimed the companies, over and above the original cost of the land, over and above the cost of bringing the water upon the land and repairs to them, have a clear profit of from $5 to $8. Then they are still obliged to pay from 25 cents to $2 per acre for the running expenses of ditches, making the actual cost less than $10 per acre. This is what it means to have the lands pass into the hands of monopolies developed in that state. We have a number of such instances where lands have been ceded to the states. Notably in California, where the lands went in a very short time into the control of corporations and monopolies. Suppose these lands were ceded to the State, and that the State Legislature would administer them in the interests of the people. It is very flattering to our self-respect. But now, gentlemen, in this case it is one of the facts of experience that when trusts have been committed to the legislatures of the states they have not always been true to the interests of the people, and the monopolies have gained strong foothold. I call your attention to a very peculiar difficulty which concerns the irrigation of this land by the Legislature. Do you suppose a Legislature would be selected, in the event of the lands being ceded, of men who are not personally interested in having the lands ceded to the State? This question is comparatively a new one and one which calls for the highest wisdom, and should not be settled without much discussion, so that the true interests of our country may be served.

Mr. Z. T. Burton, of Choteau: I am not here with any purpose of talking to you in a spread eagle style. I am here to talk on a plain practical question. On this question of not being afraid to trust this matter to future legislatures of this State, that will do for Fourth of July orations. We are here for the purpose of settling this question whether we want the government to give us these lands. We represent the State of Montana, and are not to consult the wishes of the people of other states. Our object is to encourage irrigation. Now who is going to build the water ways? It is very well to talk about future legislatures, and it is very well to talk about appropriations from Congress, but I want to say here and now that I don't believe Congress will ever build an irrigating canal in this State. The canals will be built not by Congress or the State, but by private individuals engaged in that work. It takes money and brains to build irrigation enterprises. We have got to look at this question from a practical standpoint. This State has not the money to manage that colossal land grant of some 17,000,000 acres. It will take $2,000,000 to $3,000,000 to get the land into condition.

A. J. Seligman, of Lewis and Clarke: I appreciate this subject as a business man, and am thoroughly with the expression that our first duty is toward the State. I cannot see what positive good is to come from this Salt Lake Convention, and have yet failed to see any good reasons for adopting that platform. The accepting of these lands by the State is a very serious proposition. It will require the establishment of a great many new land offices and will develop a number of political questions. And the matter of taxes is a very serious one to our taxpayers. We do not want our taxes increased.

Mr. Melton, of Beaverhead: If this irrigation problem is to be solved it must be done by the men on the ground. We are not here to wage war against any man. We are here for the purpose of finding out what is best to do, and to do it; that is the question. The Salt Lake platform is not an invaluable guide.

R. H. Howey, of Lewis and Clarke: When we come to vote on accepting these lands we are voting for the overturning of a land system that has been established for a hundred years. There has not been anything that has done so much for the country as the landed policy. Our government has established these liberal land laws which have given so many homes to citizens of the land and aided in upbuilding a great country. It is for the advocates of this measure to show the wisdom of overturning such a policy and turning a great domain over to the legislatures of seventeen states. I believe the people who have come here and made their homes here are the people who can best solve this question for themselves.

Samuel Word, of Lewis and Clarke: I am not posted on the subject of irrigation, but must confess that after listening to some of the speakers I have felt like irrigating. If any one expects that I am going to make an argument upon this question that will be interesting I am glad of it, because I find myself on both sides of the proposition. I cannot say that I am entirely in accord with the Salt Lake resolutions. I am ready to take any land that the government will cede to the State. I object to the first resolution because it asks the government to put restrictions on the lands. I am not afraid that Montana cannot take care of them. Let us take them. If we are afraid of ourselves let us substitute for this resolution, "For God's sake don't give us any lands; we don't want them."

The Committee of the Whole decided to recommend the adoption of the substitute offered by Mr. Strevell, of Custer County.

EVENING SESSION.

The Convention was called to order at 8:20 p. m.

Mr. Chisholm, Chairman of the Committee of the Whole, submitted the following report:

Mr. Chairman and Gentlemen of the Convention:—I have the honor to report that previous to its adjournment the Committee of the Whole recommended the adoption of Mr. Strevell's substitute for Article 1 of the Salt Lake platform.

On motion of Mr. Strevell, of Custer County, the substitute was adopted.

Mr. Sutherlin, of Meagher, presented the following resolution, which was adopted:

Resolved, That the next Legislature of the State of Montana be memorialized to enact a law similar in its provisions to the Wright Irrigation Law of California for the furtherance of the interests of farmers in the matter of constructing reservoirs and irrigation canals and the government of the distribution of the water.

Mr. Burton, of Choteau moved, and it was carried, that the resolutions offered by Mr. Botkin, of Lewis and Clarke, which were referred to the Committee on Resolutions, be referred back to the Committee of the Whole.

On motion of Mr. Strevell the Convention went into committee of the whole.

The resolution offered by Mr. Botkin, of Lewis and Clarke, concerning the taxation of irrigating ditches, was taken up.

Mr. Irvine, of Silver Bow, stated that the delegates from that county were to be guided in the matter by the members representing the agricultural districts, and that they had come to the Convention with that idea.

On motion of A. J. Seligman the Chairman was instructed to recommend to the Convention that the resolution be indefinitely postponed.

Mr. Sutherlin, of Meagher, introduced the following, which was recommended for adoption:

Resolved, That the next Legislature of the State of Montana be memorialized to enact a law similar in its provisions to the Wright Irrigation Law of California, for the furtherance of the interests of the farmers in the matter of constructing reservoirs and irrigating canals, and the government of the distribution of the waters.

Mr. Weed, of Lewis and Clarke, introduced the following, which was adopted:

WHEREAS, There will be held in the year 1892 a National Irrigation Congress to be attended by delegates from all the States and Territories of the arid region of the United States; and

WHEREAS, The place where such Congress shall be held has not been fixed, and is to be designated by the Executive Committee of said Congress, consisting of one delegate from each of the arid States and Territories; and

WHEREAS, Montana has within its boundaries more acres of land susceptible of irrigation, and more water available for irrigation purposes, than any other State or Territory; therefore, be it

Resolved, That the State Irrigation Convention of the State of Montana, assembled in the city of Helena, extends to the National Irrigation Congress, through its Executive Committee, a cordial and unanimous invitation to hold its annual session for the year 1892 in the State of Montana.

The committee arose and reported.

In Convention the report of the Committee of the Whole was adopted.

Mr. Strevell: Mr. President, I move that the Secretary of this Convention be and hereby is requested to transmit to the Senators and Representatives in Congress from this State the resolution which has been adopted by this Convention as a substitute for the first resolution of the Salt Lake platform, and that such action be authenticated by the President of this Convention and be transmitted at the earliest practicable day. Carried.

A motion asking for the appointment of a State Engineer, whose duties would be to guard the distribution of waters for irrigation, report upon the capacity of streams for irrigating purposes, report upon the growth of the uses of waters of rivers and streams and generally collect data upon all subjects relating to works of engineering of interest to the State and its inhabitants, was introduced.

It was moved and seconded that this motion be indefinitely postponed. Carried.

Mr. Gregory, of Gallatin: Mr. President, I move that when this Convention adjourns they adjourn to take up the subject of irrigation under a special order of business, and that the question of considering the state of irrigation in the various counties be then discussed, each county making a special report on the subject. Carried.

The President: I announce the hour of a quarter after eleven as the time to take up the special order of business called for in this motion.

Moved and seconded that a committee of one member from each county be appointed, who shall report a recommendation as to what city in Montana the National Irrigation Congress shall be invited to assemble in 1892. Carried.

Adjourned until 10 a. m. Saturday.

SATURDAY MORNING, JAN. 9.

The Convention was called to order at 10 a. m.

Mr. Meyers, Chairman of the Invitation Committee, reported as follows: "Your committee charged to select a town to invite the National Irrigation Congress next summer to hold its deliberations have performed their labors, and recommend that this Convention name the city of Helena."

After several ballots the Convention selected the town of Anaconda as the place to which to invite the National Irrigation Congress.

AFTERNOON SESSION.

The Convention was called to order at 2 p. m. by Chairman Hauser.

An invitation was read by the Secretary, inviting the members of the Convention to witness the working, at 7:30 P. M., of an Egyptian screw exhibited at 7 Main street.

Mr. Clark, of Silver Bow, introduced the following resolution:

> WHEREAS, This Convention has heard with interest the reports from different parts of this State in reference to the matter of artesian wells now in active flow in different localities, therefore be it
>
> *Resolved*, That this Convention earnestly urge upon our Senators and Representatives in Congress to use every effort to secure as large an appropriation as possible for the purpose of testing the question as to the practicability of this manner of water supply for this State, the money to be used in the actual sinking of wells, and not in expensive theorizing.

The resolution was adopted.

Mr. Wade introduced the following resolution:

> *Resolved*, That it is the sense of this Convention that our Senators and Representatives in Congress be requested to implore and, if possible, secure large appropriations for public surveys in Montana, this State having at present but one-fifth of its land surveyed, 70,000,000 acres being yet unsurveyed.
>
> *Resolved*, That we believe it will best subserve the interests of this State if no appropriation whatever be made under the direction of Major Powell, of the government geological survey, for the State of Montana. But we do ask for an appropriation for scientific research under a state department of agriculture, whereby knowledge of much value to this State may be obtained and a complete record of all moneys expended be made.

A Delegate: Mr. President, I move the adoption of this resolution.

The resolution was adopted.

Mr. Cree introduced the following resolution:

Resolved, That the thanks of this State Irrigation Convention are hereby extended to the citizens of Helena, to the members of the press, the railway officials and to the Montana Club for their kindness and for the courtesies extended to it by them.

Mr. Clark, of Silver Bow: Mr. President, I move that the Secretary read the second and third resolutions of the Salt Lake platform.

Seconded and carried.

The Secretary then read the two resolutions called for, as follows:

Resolved, That it is the sense of this Convention that the committee selected to propose and present to Congress the memorial of this Convention respecting public lands should ask as a preliminary to the cession of all lands in the territories, in accordance with the resolutions of this Convention, a liberal grant to said territories and to the states to be formed therefrom of the public lands to be devoted to public school purposes.

Resolved, That the representatives of all the states and territories directly interested in irrigation do hereby pledge their unwavering support to the just demand of such settlers; that the general government shall donate at least a portion of the funds received from the sale of such lands toward the procurement of the means necessary for their irrigation.

Mr. Clark: Mr. President, I move the adoption of these two resolutions.

This motion, having received a second, was regularly put and carried.

Mr. Gregory: Mr. President, I desire to introduce the following resolution, which the Secretary will please read:

Resolved, That the Secretary of this Convention is hereby instructed to prepare a report of the proceedings of this Convention, embracing, besides the routine business, also the speeches and particularly the important features and statistics of all the agricultural and irrigation reports from the several counties represented, and the delegates reporting on such facts are requested to send in writing the substance of such reports to the Secretary; and that this Convention do provide for the compilation and printing of the same, and for this purpose a committee be hereby appointed to do the work of compilation and see to the publication of the same.

The resolution was adopted.

Mr. Weed: Mr. President, I move that a vote of

thanks be extended to the President and other officers of this Convention for the services which they have so cheerfully rendered.

Carried.

Mr. Clark: Mr. President, I move that each county be requested to pay their pro rata share of the expense of the compiling and printing the proceedings of this Convention.

Carried.

W. E. Cullen, Lewis and Clarke: Mr. President, I desire to introduce the following resolution:

> *Resolved*, That a committee of five be appointed by the Chair, to be known as the Committee on Legislation, the duties of which committee shall be to prepare and submit to the next Legislative Assembly of the State of Montana such bills as in their judgment may tend to encourage the construction of canals and reservoirs for irrigation purposes; and that the committee, as a part of its duty, take in charge the matters set forth in the resolution offered by Mr. Bradford and that offered by Mr. Sutherlin.

The President then named the following permanent committees:

On Publication—E. D. Weed, W. C. Child and B. Brown, of Lewis and Clarke.

On Legislation—W. H. Sutherlin, Meagher; J. A. Browne, Beaverhead; G. E. Ingersoll, Cascade; J. W. Strevell, Custer; William Flannery, Gallatin.

On motion the President appointed a committee of one from each county to perfect a permanent organization of the Montana Irrigation Convention, as follows: Joseph A. Browne, Beaverhead; Z. T. Burton, Choteau; W. B. S. Higgins, Custer; H. P. Rolfe, Cascade; George Mc-Comb, Dawson; C. K. Hardenbrook, Deer Lodge; S. S. Hobson, Fergus; J. W. Caldwell, Gallatin; W. C. Child, Lewis and Clarke; Henry Whaley, Meagher; A. G. England, Missoula. R. O. Hickman, Madison; B. F. Shuart, Yellowstone; E. G. Brooke, Jefferson.

On motion of Mr. Love, of Jefferson, the Convention adjourned sine die.

APPENDIX

Showing the State of Irrigation in the Counties.

CUSTER COUNTY.

To present at this time a report on irrigation in Custer County which would describe fully or accurately her various ditches, artesian wells, irrigation pumps and other irrigation works would require more statistical work and time than it has been practicable to devote. Custer County is situated in the southeast corner of the State of Montana, and comprises a vast domain, over a hundred by a hundred and thirty-five miles square. The irrigation enterprises alluded to are situated in various sections of the county, many of them partially completed and others under construction.

The largest ditch now in operation in the county is that owned and operated by the Miles City Irrigating and Ditch Company, which has cost about $100,000. The head gate is situated fourteen miles from Miles City, where the water is taken from Tongue River by means of a permanent dam, constructed entirely across the stream, raising the water some twelve feet above its natural bed. This ditch has a capacity at present of 3,000 inches, and is completed for twenty miles. There is sufficient water retained by this company's dam to enable them to extend their ditch to twice its length and enlarge its carrying capacity three or four times and still have abundance of water to draw upon. There is lying under this canal 30,000 to 35,000 acres of good productive soil, only 1,500 to 2,000 acres of which are as yet being irrigated and improved. These lands alluded to as good and productive, when viewed in their natural state are as uninviting and unpromising as could well be found, but when water is applied our native blue stem (than which no better forage plant exists) immediately springs up. So phenomenal has been the success of the first users of the waters of this canal that the adjacent lands are being rapidly bought and the sage and grease wood removed, so that 1892 will see one to two thousand acres added to the amount as above under cultivation.

The next largest ditch, and the largest private enterprise of this kind in our county, is situated on the head waters of the Rosebud, owned and operated by Hubbard & Thompson, who irrigate 1,500 to 1,800 acres of native hay, alfalfa, corn, oats, barley, and such garden crops as tomatoes, potatoes, melons, okra, egg plant, oyster plant, etc., etc. Their entire system of ditches comprise nearly thirty miles in length, the smallest being six feet at top and four feet at bottom, carrying a depth of ten inches of water, the larger being ten feet at top and eight feet at bottom, fifteen inches deep. The total cost of this work, including fencing and reclaiming the land, which would have remained absolutely worthless without irrigation, has been in this case about $10 to $12 per acre.

On the north side of the Yellowstone, in the western part of our county, a ditch ten feet at top and seven feet at bottom, and some eight miles long, is under construction, and promises speedy completion. This ditch is designed to irrigate what is known as Pease Bottom, one of the most beautiful sections of the great Yellowstone valley, comprising more than 18,000 acres.

Below Miles City ten miles, and on the north side of the Yellowstone, is being constructed a canal, several miles of which are already graded, and a large amount of work also has been done at its head, near the mouth of Sunday creek, where the waters to supply it is being taken out of the Yellowstone. This ditch, when completed, will be eleven miles in length and carry 5,000 inches of water. Less than $5,000 will be required to complete it, as the heavy cutting for two miles and more, at its head, is already finished, the balance of the work being shallow and comparatively inexpensive.

Howes, Strevell & Miles have constructed on Otter creek, a tributary of Tongue river, ditches and laterals comprising some twelve miles, with three quite expensive dams. These ditches so far have been used chiefly to irrigate pasture lands and alfalfa.

On Little Pumpkin creek, sixty miles south of Miles City, is to be found one of the oldest and possibly, capacity considered, one of the most inexpensive ditches in our county. This ditch is but little over a mile in length, but carries over sixty inches of water. It was constructed and is owned and operated by Mr. James Davidson, whose green pastures and meadows in summer and immense hay ricks in winter testify to the richness of our soil and inestimable advantages of irrigation.

On upper Tongue river Mr. Joseph Scott has completed a ditch some three miles in length, and in width fifteen feet at top and nine feet at bottom. From this ditch Mr. Scott irrigates some 720 acres, principally hay land. Its capacity is sufficient to ultimately supply water for nearly two thousand acres of land lying under it, which is entirely barren without irrigation. Its cost was $3,500.

Next to our ditches, in line of irrigation improvements, we may mention vacuum steam pumps, which the citizens of this county are pioneers (in Montana) in introducing, as a means of raising water for irrigation at points where the taking out of ditches seemed impracticable, but where small bodies of good land can be found and water abundant. Many such locations are found along the Yellowstone and upon smaller tributaries of various streams.

Two years ago Bolles & Co., of Rosebud, placed one of these pumps and operated it as an experiment. The volume of water discharged was so great and the expense of fuel so slight that no less than six of our citizens, among whom are Messrs. Scott, Cree, Barringer, Laney and others, men widely known in this State, have purchased and put in position, for use the coming summer, pumps of this kind. The pump used by Mr. Cree last year was found equal to filling a ditch with capacity to thoroughly irrigate some three hundred acres. Mr. Barringer has in place for use this season a mammoth pump calculated to supply water for more than four hundred acres of plowed land, which is known to require vastly more water than turf or meadow ground. There seems to be little doubt that the pump will prove equal to the task, and its total cost will not exceed $1,800.

Last, but not least, may be noticed our artesian wells, of which we have now in use over thirty in the vicinity of Miles City alone, some of which flow several inches of water, with force to raise water fifteen to forty five feet from the surface. The lower Yellowstone valley, lying, as it does, at the comparatively low altitude of 1,500 to 2,000 feet above sea level (while nearly all of the other important agricultural valleys of the State are known to be at an altitude of 3,000 to 4,000 feet), is peculiarly favored in respect to the easy and inexpensive securing of artesian water. One well two miles from Miles City flows at two feet from the surface nearly two barrels per minute, and at an elevation of forty feet from the surface about half that quantity. This well is only 166 feet in depth, with a bore of two and one-half inches, and cost less than two hundred dollars.

As an example of what a wonder a little water worketh, a circumstance may be cited, the details of which are known to scores of our people. A Mr. Hyde purchased a two-acre lot near Miles City, the improvements consisting of a two-room house and an artesian well, the flow from which was so feeble as to be barely adequate to irrigate during the dryest seasons one to one and a half acres. The price paid was $700. Mr. Hyde commenced gardening, with the result that he realized from his investment by reason of his sales of garden produce alone never less than $1,200, and for some seasons as high as $1,600.

Recent experiments show beyond any question that with irrigation we can grow alfalfa most abundantly and profitably. In California, Arizona and New Mexico, where this forage plant is known to flourish, and is both as to soil and to climate in its element, the writer has observed, it can under best conditions be cut from four to five times per year. Here, where, prior to the advent of our canals, it was tried and declared a failure, we now cut three crops during a single season, and the yield in tons per acre is equal to the largest known elsewhere.

The same is true respecting Indian corn, heretofore considered an impossible crop in Montana and throughout the higher altitudes. In the mountainous sections extending through all of the central and western portion of the State it must remain impossible of production. Here, however, in the Yellowstone, Powder, Tongue and Little Missouri valleys, and particularly the lower Yellowstone, Indian corn as fine and maturing as early as Iowa or Missouri may be and is being grown.

Custer County's exhibit of corn and tobacco at the State Fair last August (about the 8th to 12th) was a revelation to many, including old Montanians, who were loth to believe that corn and tobacco showing a growth of twelve feet and more of stalk, and the former bearing mature ears of corn with eighteen and twenty rows of kernels around the cob, were matured in Montana at that date, if at all.

It is a fact well known in Eastern Montana that Custer County strawberries are not only beyond comparison as to quality, but that they come to maturity and are out of the market before the same fruit from Bozeman and some other sections are ready for market.

It has been said of Eastern Montana that "it is the coldest and hottest country on the globe," and to whatever of truth there may be in this observation to a considerable degree doubtless our success in growing corn, tomatoes, tobacco, small fruits, etc., is due.

A careful observer cannot fail to note that in this arid, rainless, cloudless region, spring comes earlier, and the fructifying influences of the sun are much earlier realized than in many localities farther south.

We have very little snow, and as a rule it rarely stays to the first of March. The Yellowstone, Powder, Rosebud and Big Horn rivers, the writer has observed for more than a dozen years, have broken up and cleared of ice one, two or more weeks prior to the breaking up of the Missouri, or even the Mississippi opposite Minnesota and Iowa.

There is yet unappropriated abundance of water in the Yellowstone and Powder rivers. The fall of these streams is everywhere sufficient to make construction of ditches practicable. Only the great outlay necessary has thus far deterred our inhabitants and the owners of arable lands in securing these waters. That there is a sort of wave of popular feeling throughout Montana, as well as her sister arid states, must unquestionably lead speedily and surely to the solving of the great problem. Let it be said in conclusion that none can feel more interest, none take more just pride in doing her whole duty in helping the popular movement, none hope for greater benefits than the citizens of Custer County.   J. W. STREVELL.

CHOTEAU COUNTY.

I find the total number of ditches in the southwestern portion of Choteau County to be thirty-two, with a length of sixty-five miles, and covering an area of about 30,180 acres. I find the reservoir system is only in its initiative at present, there being only five or six so far established, the smallest covering not more than half an acre, and the largest covering about forty acres, with an average depth of eight feet of water. I also find that all available water for irrigation (except the waters of the Missouri) have been appropriated by individuals and corporations during the irrigation season, and that in order to reclaim and bring under profitable cultivation all or any portion of the land now arid and uncultivated it will be necessary to resort to the reservoir system in order to store the waters when not used by prior claimants.   J. F. PATTERSON.

CASCADE COUNTY.

Cascade County contains about 3,000 square miles, mostly valley and bench lands of an average elevation of about 3,000 feet above the level of the sea. It is bounded by the Highwood and Belt mountains on the east, the Belt and Birdtail ranges on the south, with prairie lands on the north and west. It is watered by the Belt and Smith rivers and their branches, Willow and Otter creeks, Hound, Stickney, Wegner, Sand Coulee and Box Elder creeks emptying directly or indirectly into the Missouri river from the south. The Dearborn and Sun rivers and Muddy creek flow into it from the north and west side of the river. The Missouri river runs for about ninety miles in a northerly direction through the county. It conveys about double the amount of water that the Mississippi does at St. Paul.

At the falls of the Missouri at Great Falls there is 267,000 horse power developed and undeveloped, or an amount equal to all the other water power in the United States with that of Niagara added. This enormous power is already partly used in the great smelting and manufacturing plants constructed there, and could be used in raising the great volume of water of the Missouri and irrigating a large portion of Cascade, Choteau and Dawson counties. A large portion of the soil, perhaps from one-half to two-thirds, is a sandy loam extending from the Missouri river to the Belt mountains. From this vast acreage in the driest seasons we have produced from ten to twenty bushels of wheat and thirty to forty bushels of oats per acre without irrigation, amounts which would be trebled by irrigation. Last season the yield was from thirty to forty bushels of wheat, seventy-five to one hundred bushels of oats, and 250 to 300 bushels of potatoes without irrigation. All this land would, however, be improved by irrigation.

The canals already constructed here have cost about $500,000, and including laterals and small ditches would make about 400 to 500 miles. The main canal of the Cascade Land Company, taken out of the North Fork of the Sun River and tributaries of the Teton, is about sixty-five miles in length and twelve to sixteen feet in width. It carries about 3,000 inches of water and will irrigate 3,000 acres of land. Benton lake, three miles by seven miles in extent, is used as a reservoir. During the year the company has cut about $15,000 or $20,000 worth of hay, although their system is not yet completed. In the length of the canal the lateral ditches are not counted. The Sun River ditch has been in operation many years. It is ten to twelve miles long and cost about $2,000 a mile. It carries about 3,000 inches of water and will irrigate 3,000 acres of land On one ranch covered by this ditch the farming profits this year were over $7,000. The Crown Butte canal is twenty-six miles in length and sixteen feet in width, and cost about $3,000 a mile. It carries about 40,000 inches of water. The canal irrigates an immense body of land between the Sun river and the Missouri Wilson and Thompson are the owners of a system of reservoirs and canals at a point near the termination of the Crown Butte canal. The system comprises four immense reservoir and some twenty-four miles of canals, covering thousands of acres of land and representing an investment of $30,000. The Chestnut Valley ditch takes the waters of the Missouri at Ha'f Breed rapids. It is twelve miles in length and carries about 15,000 inches of water. The Belt Creek ditch is five miles in length and waters all land on the Lower Belt. Another ditch on Willow creek is from five to seven miles in length There are many ditches from one-half mile to one mile in length on Belt, Willow, Cora, Otter, Sand Coulee, Deep and Wegner creeks and in other localities, the number of which it is impossible to compute. Two canals have been surveyed on Lower Sun river from Priest rapids. Each one will be twelve miles in length and run on each side of the river. Surveys were made for similarly located canals as long ago as 1876 at the time the Missour River Navigation company was formed. On Hound creek and Smith river another large canal is projected and to be built this spring which will be from fifteen to twenty miles in length and irrigate lands along the Smith river and east of the Missouri river.

DEER LODGE COUNTY.

Deer Lodge County is a mountainous district intersected by the Deer Lodge, Flint Creek, Nevada Creek and Big Blackfoot valleys, which contain nearly all of the agricultural land in the county. These valleys are traversed lengthwise by streams bearing their names. This section constitutes the watershed of the Clark's Fork of the Columbia river. The valleys are drained latterly by a large number of small streams, the waters of which have all been appropriated by the settlers along the same. There are in the county 460 ditches, conveying the water an aggregate distance of about 750 miles, or an average of less than two miles each, and having a carrying capacity of about 85,000 miner's inches and irrigating about 95,000 acres. During the high water in June of an average water season there is a supply of water more than sufficient to fill the ditches already constructed, but during dry seasons, such as 1889 and 1890, and all seasons after the high water time, there is not enough in the natural flow of the streams to supply the present demand. There being about 350,000 acres of land susceptable of irrigation in the county, it is apparent that some artificial means must be used to make these lands available for settlement. It is also apparent that if the waters which are constantly flowing out of the county during the high water season and during the time that they are not used in the ditches could be utilized there would be plenty for all future demands. There are at the sources of nearly all of the streams in the county, basins and natural lakes varying from one-fourth of a mile to several square miles in extent, which might be readily turned into reservoirs for the storage of the surplus water. This would not be altogether an experiment. The Rock Creek Ditch company, operating the placer mines at Pioneer, constructed a reservoir several years ago by drifting in and tapping the Rock Creek lake fifteen feet below the surface of the water. Then a dam fourteen feet high was built across the outlet to retain the waste water, thus giving them a body of water twenty-nine feet deep, one mile long and one-half mile wide, from which a good head of water is drawn. Nature has furnished us with water in abundance; it remains for capital and muscle to utilize it so that every acre of the land in this county may be reclaimed.

C. K. HARDENBROOK.

DAWSON COUNTY.

Dawson County is the northeastern county of the State, is about 155 miles from north to south and 175 miles from east to west; an area of 26,820 square miles, or a little over seventeen millions of acres. A large part of this vast area consists of rolling uplands, covered with bunch and buffalo grasses, suitable for grazing of cattle, horses and sheep, and which are too high above the water courses to be available for the purposes of irrigation.

The county is traversed from west to east for nearly two-hundred miles by the valley of the Missouri river, which divides the county into two nearly equal parts, and in the southern part of the county the Yellowstone, flowing in a northeasterly course, runs for something over a hundred miles within our borders. Branches of these two large rivers flow into them both on the north and south, and in the spring and early summer pour out vast quantities of water which they drain from the broken and rolling country forming the divides between the great rivers.

It is in the broad valleys of the Yellowstone and Missouri rivers, and on the bottoms lying along the smaller streams, that are found the lands which, when irrigated and made fertile by the water now flowing to waste by them, will make eastern Montana the garden of the whole northwest.

At the present time there is but very little done in Dawson County in the line of irrigation; a few small private ditches, conveying water to a few hundred acres of land is all that can be called, by any stretch of the imagination, irrigation. The reason for this is that our best farming lands are not situated in such a way as to be easily and cheaply irrigated by small and inexpensive ditches taken from mountain streams, as in some other counties of the State, where every man can own his own ditch or a few farmers can club together and construct one suited to their needs and for their own use.

But in Dawson County, more than in any other locality in the State, are found opportuities for irrigation on a large scale; and when once the eyes of capital can be opened to the conditions here existing for profitable investments we look for an era of prosperity unequaled by any country that is not built up upon the substantial foundation of an agricultural population.

In the valley of the Missouri alone can be found at a low estimate one-half a million acres of good agricultural land which can be irrigated by means of canals taken from the river, and there is at all seasons of the year abundance of water for such a purpose.

Tributary to the Missouri are the Milk, Poplar, Muscleshell, Big Dry and Big Muddy rivers, besides innumerable smaller streams, which by a system of storage reservoirs can be used to irrigate the lands along their borders. The valley of the Milk river is just now, because of the settlement of that part of the county by the building of the Great Northern railway, and the attention which has been directed to that locality by the advertisement of that railroad, looked upon as a suitable place for a successful attempt at irrigating a large body of land.

But it is in the south part of the county, on the borders of the Yellowstone river, that we look for the greatest practical results in the near future. This valley, which has by some one been called the future "Mohawk Valley of Montana," is, in Dawson county, about 120 miles in length and on an average from four to five miles in width from the river to the foothills, a prairie country unrivaled in its fertility by any on earth. There is a heavy fall in the river for the whole distance, and by a system of canals, easy of construction, the whole valley can be brought into cultivation.

A movement is now on foot for the organization of a stock company at Glendive, the county seat, for the purpose of constructing a ditch to be taken from the Yellowstone river, on the north side about thirty miles above Glendive, which will irrigate about 100,000 acres, known as Lone Horse prairie. The land in this locality is all surveyed, is one-half unclaimed government land, which is open for settlement, and the other half is covered by the Northern Pacific railroad company's land grant. The railroad company has expressed a willingness to give an irrigation company all assistance in their power for the furtherance of such an undertaking, and if pushed with energy it will doubtless prove a success.

Below Glendive, from that town to the mouth of the Yellowstone river, are many places where canals can and will in the not distant future be constructed, which will reclaim hundreds of thousands of acres which are now only fit for grazing.

The lower Yellowstone valley has for the past ten or twelve years, since the first coming of the Northern Pacific railroad and the wave of immigration following in its wake, been looked upon as one of the most favorable localities for settlement, and many attempts have been made by farmers to locate and try to build up homes and make a living. But it is only in a few favorable places that they have been successful; and most of them have been compelled to leave what improvements they have made and seek homes where they can raise crops with greater certainty.

It is not claimed for the Yellowstone valley that it is a "granger's paradise," as some parts of Montana are claimed to be; but when such a system of irrigation is adopted, as it is sure to be in a few years, the far famed Gallatin must look to its laurels.

Besides the lands above mentioned, which can be irrigated by means of ditches taken from the rivers and creeks, there are many thousands of acres of valuable agricultural lands which, if as is generally conceded we are in an artesian basin, can be watered by artesian wells. If this proves to be the truth, and such irrigation proves to be practicable and comparatively inexpensive, the quantity of arable land will be of enormous extent, as there are thousands upon thousands of as yet unsurveyed lands lying on all the high benches which are equal if not superior to the bottoms and low bench lands in their capacity for producing crops.

It is very difficult to estimate the amount of lands in Dawson County which are located in such a way as to be susceptible of irrigation, for the reason that a very large portion of the county remains unsurveyed, and at the best any estimate would be simply "guess work." However, to leave a large amount of allowance for "bad lands," the following estimate will not, we think, be any too large: Lands in the Missouri valley which can be watered from the river by means of canals, 500,000 acres; bottom lands along the tributaries of the Missouri, which can be watered by a combined system of ditches and storage reservoirs, 2,000,000 acres; lands in the Yellowstone Valley which can be irrigated by ditches from the river, 250,000 acres; bench lands which can only be irrigated by wells, either artesian or for pumping, 5,000,000 acres; total, 7,750,000.

We think that from seven to eight millions of acres is a reasonable estimate of the amount of land in Dawson County which can be irrigated and made fertile as soon as the time comes when all this will be needed for settlement.

By what we have shown above it will be seen that, although Dawson cannot boast the rich mineral resources which are the birthright of many of her sister counties, still in the wealth of resource which underlies every agricultural section of the world she is rich in latent wealth; and when the time comes, as it surely will, that these millions of acres are sending to less favored parts of the State their products in return for the gold and silver of Lewis and Clarke and Silver Bow, and the other mountain counties, then and not till then will Montana occupy the high place she is destined to hold in the sisterhood of states.

FERGUS COUNTY.

Fergus County has 74,000 acres of land that is under ditch. The main ditches covering this area are 242 miles in length, the building of which has cost $160 per mile, which would make the total cost of these ditches $38,400, being a fraction over fifty cents per acre. The lands that these ditches cover are situated along the bottom land or valleys of streams. There are 17,000 acres taken up that is not yet irrigated, and 1,000,000 acres of irrigable land not yet taken that could be made productive by irrigation. The balance of the lands of the county are hilly and mountainous, and are only fit for grazing. The principal streams within the county are Judith river, Wolf creek, Big Spring and Flat Willow. The waters of these streams are already appropriated, with the exception of the overflow in high water times or such times of the year as it is not used for irrigation.

The government has reserved two sites for reservoirs on the Judith river, which are situated in the right place to cover large tracts of land not yet irrigated, but are impracticable for two reasons: First, they would be dangerous to the lives of the people living along the streams below where these reservoirs are situated. Second, reserving water in the beds of streams is not far-reaching enough in comparison to their cost of building. The beds of streams generally are narrow and with a heavy grade of fall. The water stored would be limited to a small fraction of the actual overflow in high water time. But this overflow could be carried out in canals and stored in outside basins, of which there are quite a number to be found in Fergus County.   JAMES ETTIEN.

GALLATIN COUNTY.

The mileage of private farm ditches in the Gallatin valley, i. e., the cultivable portion of Gallatin County, Mont., it would be exceedingly difficult to give. Some attempt, however, must be made in order that a stranger to the situation may form a tolerably correct idea of the extent of irrigation in this locality.

Hundreds of miles of private farm ditches exist; these come out of some twenty or more creeks and streams, including the East Gallatin river—a small feeder to the West Gallatin, which latter is a strong mountain stream of heavy fall to the mile, and of large capacity of flowage, which I will state later on; so that portions of more than a dozen townships are supplied, more or less, with irrigation facilities, and some thoroughly. This valley, so far as the cultivable area is concerned, may be roughly said to be four townships wide by five townships long, allowing great sinuosity on the marginal exteriors, mainly sloping with undulations from south to north, with counter slopes from the circumference; everywhere surrounded by mountainous country, which is indented with deep cuts or canyons on the easterly and southerly borders, from which issue permanently flowing streams. From all these streams except the West Gallatin river every drop of water is conducted into small and large private farm ditches, and utilized for irrigation. From the West Gallatin river, also, many ditches are taken for farm use; from this river alone are taken out the three large canals owned by incorporated companies, named in order of time of construction, the Gallatin Canal Company, the West Gallatin Irrigation Company, and the Excelsior Canal Company.

By far the greater part of the water of this river runs to waste; it is many times in its flowage the volume of all the water taken into its tapping ditches.

There are no reservoirs of water in this valley, from which conserved waters are drawn. Up the Bozeman canyon there is Mystic lake, some fourteen miles from Bozeman, some 2,000 feet in height.

above this valley, where a dam twenty-two feet high is being built now to hold back water, to be run down the natural channel of great and rapid fall, and then to be drawn off into ditches for foothill and bench-land irrigation. The capacity of this pond may be understood from its size, about one mile long by one-half mile wide, and great depth may be secured.

The only land companies are the Manhattan Malting Company and the West Gallatin Irrigation Company, the latter constructing a large canal to supply water to its own lands, and grantees of its land and still owning some 25,000 acres; the former owning 160 acres in townsite at Manhattan and some 10,000 acres for its own farming purposes, mainly for the cultivation of barley.

The Gallatin Canal Company's ditch is twenty miles long; cost said to be about $60,000; built about three years ago; taken out of the east side of the West Gallatin river, well up to the canyon; carries about 8,000 inches, it is said; built with inexpensive headgate and wing sieve dam of no great cost.

The Excelsior Canal Company's ditch is twelve miles long; built in 1890-91; cost about $40,000, as estimated, and built by syndicate of farm owners under it, supplying water to its stockholders only; carries about 8,000 inches, it is stated; built with slight structure of headgate, and no dam.

The largest and most costly canal is that of the West Gallatin Irrigation Company, constructed 1890-91, and at present some twenty-four miles in length, on a high line to cover bench lands; taken out of the west side of the West Gallatin river; still in process of extension in length.

Location.—The canal is taken out of the West Gallatin river near the centre of Sec. 28 3S 4E., Montana, and runs through sections 28, 21, 16, 9 and 4 in 3S 4E., and through sections 23, 33, 27, 28, 21, 22, 16, 17, 20, 19 and 18 in 2S 4E., ending near the centre of Sec. 13, 1S 4E., about twenty-four miles from its head. A plat and profile of the canal show it to be very crooked, and the ground is more tortuous than the plat, because there are many short and sharp turns that could not be shown on a plat of small scale. This was necessary in following the contour of such a rough and broken country as most of the canal is built over, which is a succession of long ridges and deep gulches, pointing in a general direction toward the northwest.

Dimensions.—Canal is finished to twenty-four miles. The first 1,300 feet from the head is twenty-four feet on the bottom, and from there to the twenty-third mile is narrowed to fourteen feet on the bottom, but widens in many places to sixteen and eighteen feet. The narrowest place on the bottom anywhere in the whole twenty and a half miles is full fourteen feet, twenty-three and a quarter miles from the head, and the next three miles is wider and shallower, but is intended to carry the same amount of water as the rest of the ditch.

Grade.—Is constructed on a fall of 6-100 to 100 feet, or three feet to a mile, except the first 1,300 feet below the head has a fall of two and a half feet in the 1,300 feet, or over ten feet to a mile.

Slopes.—Are one to one, except in solid rock, where it is one-half to one.

Banks.—Are from five to eight feet high above the bottom of the canal, and are from twenty-five to forty-five feet wide at their base, solid and firm, and slope evenly on both sides. All the earth and rock from excavating the canal is placed on the lower side (on the north and east), as nearly the whole length of the canal is built on side hills.

Headgate.—Is twenty-four feet wide in the clear, with five gates, built of timber 10x12 and 8x12, well braced and bolted, and most thoroughly built throughout. The bottom of the head-gate being four feet below the surface of the river at the present low state of water, which, with the two and a half foot fall 'n the first 1,300 feet, makes the canal capable of receiving water fully five feet deep in it should it ever be required. There is no dam.

Flumes.—Are all built of heavy square and two-inch plank, in the most thorough manner.

Tunnel.—In the ninth mile from the head is a tunnel, 241 feet in length, and is five and a half feet deep by twelve feet wide, with a fall of 60-100 feet to 100 feet; timbered a little at each end, balance solid rock; highest point of ground above bottom of tunnel is forty-seven feet; distance around the hill or spur from upper end of tunnel to its lower end is 4,750 feet, the tunnel making a saving of distance of 4,509 feet.

The canal will carry water four feet deep, and could very easily be made to carry four and a half feet. In this canal, fourteen feet wide on the bottom, slope one to one, water four feet deep, with its grade of three feet fall to the mile, will flow 10,695 miners' inches of water, from which will have to be deducted a reasonable per cent. for seepage and evaporation.

Remarks.—This canal will carry 3,510 more miners' inches of water than one twelve feet wide on the bottom, slope of one to one, water three and one-half feet deep, grade two and one-half feet to the mile.

The most of the country over which it is built is very rough and broken, its location coming on steep side hills and around and over deep gulches. The grade is maintained even, and all slopes made as smooth as possible with pick and shovel, and no rock or coarse gravel left in the bottom, thus reducing the friction of the water on the wetted perimeter of the canal to the lowest minimum, thereby reducing the loss from that cause and increasing the flow of water.

The canal from end to end in all particulars is most thoroughly and honestly built, showing in every foot of its length that it was made with the view of it being permanent and lasting, and to carry a large volume of water. The cost of this canal so far is about $90,000.

In this connection it is not important to state the area cultivated under these canals separately. Under the two first named canals the total capacity of the ditches is required for the ground under them, and such land is already mostly in cultivation; under the last-named ditch the lands are mainly new and unbroken, and are just brought into such relation to water as to be cultivable. There lie under this ditch, as it may be extended, sixty thousand acres, being more than the ditch has capacity to supply with water.

With caution held out that an estimate must be considered something of a guess, I should say that under great and little ditches there are about 50,000 acres in cultivation, under crops in one year, and in this I am not counting the fallow ground of that year.

The Auditor's report for Montana for 1890 gives the number of ranches in Gallatin County at 460, and the acreage in ranches in Gallatin County as 127,684 acres, and the ranches fenced as 115,374 acres. No scrutiny is made in these returns into the number of acres plowed. The acreage and number of ranches have increased considerably since such figures were made up, and these figures are returns for assessment purposes only and include railroad lands cultivated or uncultivated in the county. Much of such lands may not be cultivated. No such return is an index of what is cultivated area; let us go, therefore, to crop returns. The crop returns in the Auditor's report are not to be relied upon as coming up to the magnitude of area or yield per acre. We know individually of one tract of 1,200 acres now in cultivation, not embraced in 1890 year returns; we know of several tracts of 100 acres and upward, brought recently under the plow, not in such estimates. Fifty thousand acres are assumed as proximately the area in cultivation over and above what is fallow, i. e., it is approximately the area cropped in a year. Taking the crops and hay and the vegetable and small fruit crops, and we may assume a yield of $1,250,000 in value. There are thirty-five threshing machines here. These may be estimated as threshing 60,000 bushels each, on the average. This gives 2,100,000 bushels.

The average price of the three staples I place at an assumed figure, which I am advised is fair, and from this I get $1,250,000 as a year's yield in value.

These figures are less than some stated statistics in advertisements of this famous valley.

To mark on a map all the ditches would be to run out tortuous lines from every creek and river as thick as branches and their twigs from the main stem of a tree. A great fertile expanse, gridironed with circumfluent lines of ditches, bright and golden in harvest time with grain, and hay meadows in green for relief, and after harvest with stubble as a plush carpet is with its short, upreared filaments, is not an overdrawn picture of this valley.

Barley is great in yield and supreme in quality here; oats triumph in weight and measure to the acre, and wheat yield is as high in average as in any known region. A little table of crop reports of 1891, printed without selection or partiality, just as made by chance returns from ranchers for neighborhood use, is printed by the Bozeman *Avant Courier*.

You ask for the price of water. Water is not retailed here, but the price as understood by the canal companies is $2 per statutory inch as measured in accordance with the statutes of Montana. This is a reasonable price, per year.

Prices of crops paid to farmers in 1890 is about this: Average oats, stated about $1.50 cwt.; average barley, stated about $1.15 cwt.; average soft wheat, stated about 75 cents per bushel; hard wheat, 85 cents per bushel; No. 1 timothy hay, about $14 per ton; wild hay, about $2 to $2.50 per ton less than timothy. Oats sometimes as high as from $2 to $2.10; barley, sometimes as high as $1.55 per cwt.; hay, $14 per ton.

The crop of 1891 was large and the following are some of the returns: M. H. Allen, twenty-four acres of oats, 3,100 bushels; 129 bushels to the acre. J. H. Gallo[...] acres of wheat, 6,800 bushels; sixty-five bushels to the acre. Z[...] Morgan, 300 acres wheat, 16,381 bushels; fifty-four bushels to the acre. William B. Reed, 213 acres oats, 20,251 bushels; ninety-five bushels to the acre. M. H. Penwell, 450 acres wheat and oats, 23,383 bushels; fifty-one bushels to the acre. Wm. Flannery, 575 acres wheat and oats, 30,950 bushels, fifty-four bushels to the acre.

This shows a few representative crops; these are not given as average samples, and would exceed the average.

Gallatin County produces, approximately, about one-third of the cereals of the State.

There are in the Gallatin valley proper, approximately, 350,000 acres of arable land, and in the county about 400,000 acres. To irrigate this, there are in the valley 100,000 inches of water outside of the main West Gallatin river, which has 300,000 additional inches. This is an estimate, and exactness is not to be expected, and we take the water at its high stage in irrigation season.

That part of the agricultural area on the Madison and Jefferson rivers is amply supplied with water from those streams.

In closing, I am advised that there is an ample supply of water flowing in this valley and county to irrigate all the area that is cultivable, supposing proper provision is made for running the water to the plow lands. C. A. GREGORY.

LEWIS AND CLARKE COUNTY.

There are practically six irrigation valleys in Lewis and Clarke County, containing nearly all of the available farming land. First is the valley of the Big Prickly Pear, in which is situated the Capital of the State. This valley is fourteen miles in width and about sixteen in length. While all of this is fine farming land, it is not available because of the lack of water. There are, however, about 10,000 acres under irrigation, deriving its supply of water from the Big Prickly Pear creek. In this area are some of the finest farms in the State. The magnificent farm owned by Mr. W. C. Child eclipses all other farms in the Northwest. Mr. Child has under fence about 2,000 acres, irrigated by a perfect system of ditches. In connection with his farming ditches is a water power generating fifty horse power, with which he grinds feed for several hundred head of thoroughbred stock and furnishes power for a very complete creamery, wherein is to be found all the latest machinery for separating cream from new milk and immediately turning it into butter. Mr. Child has erected in addition to his creamery a barn costing $25,000, in the basement of which he stables about 500 milch cows. In the second story are enormous bins containing grain and other feed.

Among the other valuable farms of this system may be mentioned the fine horse and grain farm of W. G. Preuitt, Secretary of the Montana Live Stock Association. This farm contains about 1,000 acres and is under a very high state of cultivation. The large farm known as "Lowlands," belonging to Mr. Donald Bradford, is an example of what may be done with Montana soil, well irrigated. "Lowlands" embraces 1,000 acres of very rich wash loam, that produces an average grain crop of 60 bushels and 250 bushels of potatoes. Lower down the Prickly Pear hay ranches predominate, producing from two to three tons of blue joint and other valuable hay grasses per acre. Upon Ten-Mile creek the farm of Mr. John J. Fant is situated. This farm contains about 640 acres and produces rich crops of hay and grain.

The Little Prickly Pear valley lies northwest of Helena about twenty-five miles. Irrigation is used only to a limited extent in this valley, the soil being impregnated with water from springs. The important hay crops are nourished without the aid of ditches. This fact enabled the use of the waters of the Little Prickly Pear creek on lands situated upon a rising plateau running towards the City of Helena. This scheme embraces about 2,000 acres.

Rock Creek basin, lying between the Little Prickly Pear and Dearborn valleys, includes several rich farms, the most important being that of Mr. D. A. G. Floweree, containing 1,700 acres. Mr. Floweree constructed just above his farm a reservoir that catches the spring waters of Rock creek, distributing them during the season of irrigation. This reservoir is the most complete in Lewis and Clarke

County, if not in the State. North of this is situated the Dearborn canal system. The Dearborn valley is richly endowed with every attribute of wealth. Comprising all that territory bounded on the south by the picturesque Dearborn river, on the north by the Sun river, on the east by the Missouri river, and upon the west by the main range of the Rocky Mountains, it is a splendid arrangement of nature. Its topographical features are unique, the valley being divided into four separate and distinct slopes, all of them deriving their water for irrigation from the Dearborn river, the waters of which are diverted about one and one-half miles above the mouth of the Grand Canyon of the Dearborn and conveyed by means of the Dearborn canal to Summit Lake, from which point the water is conveyed by smaller canals to the heads of the streams known as Flat creek, Auchard creek, Dry creek and Simms' creek. Each of these creeks runs down the center of a narrow valley and distributes the waters to the ditches belonging to the farms lying along its course. All the territory between these streams is undulating, furnishing the settlers in the valleys a magnificent pasture free of cost and immediately at their doors. Its water rights are perfect, the company having absolute control of the whole Dearborn river. Its water supply is first-class, with a reservoir system covering 5,000 acres, at an average depth of forty feet. The main canal is 38 feet wide, 6 feet depth of water, and has a grade of 3.1 feet per mile. Its whole construction is based upon safety and utility, without regard to cost. Its dam and head gates are, combined, 300 feet in length, and have withstood the onslaught of the greatest of spring floods. The main reservoir will be independent of the canal supply and outlet, thus insuring the settlers against the lack of water because of breaks in either the canal or reservoirs. These reservoirs will hold sufficient water to supply every acre of farming land in the valley during the whole season of irrigation. Thus it will be seen the settlers are safe from drought beyond a peradventure.

Recognizing the naturally adverse interests existing between the owners of canals and the users of water, the management has originated and will put into practice the plan of organizing the farmers of each creek's slope, district or valley into associations, such association to elect its own water master or superintendent, who shall receive the waters from the canal management and distribute them in the way desired by the farmers. A board of trustees, composed of farmers, shall pass upon all disputes as between the farmers and shall manage the building of laterals and the distribution of waters through the water master. They shall assess benefits, collect water rents aed settle with the canal management for the water. In this way there will be no conflicts between the canal company and the farmers. The water will be delivered to and measured through weirs at given points and paid for in advance according to such measurement. This board of trustees shall be elected by the owners of the lands irrigated the next preceding year, each voter to have as many votes as he had acres irrigated. New irrigators or those desiring to increase their area of land to be irrigated may become voters providing they contract for the necessary water to cover the acreage commanding the votes. The company will establish a price per cubic foot per second. The trustees will decide upon the quantity of water necessary for the land and purchase from the company accordingly. This will insure economy in the use of water and will enable the company, because of such economy, to cover a larger area.

The results will be economy both for the consumers and the company, no conflicts, no irritation, a greater number of acres irrigated.

The officers of this canal are L. U S. Ames, President; Henry Semple Ames, Vice President; Donald Bradford, General Manager; general offices, Helena, Montana.

With the exception of Big Prickly Pear valley, the whole of Lewis and Clarke County is well supplied with water and will be quickly occupied by settlers of a superior class. Its markets are the best in the Northwest, as it is close to the three largest and most important cities, and it has direct railroad connection with every mining camp.

MADISON COUNTY.

The Madison and Jefferson rivers, with the tributaries of the latter stream, such as the Big Hole, Beaverhead and the Ruby rivers, furnish the principal water supply of Madison County, and have their source high up near the main range of the Rocky Mountains. With the discovery of the famous placer mines of Alder Gulch early in the year 1863, which caused a heavy influx of population and settled the valleys, the large mining industry that sprang into existence in a day created a demand for all farm products, which had to be supplied at that time from the valleys of Utah, and although the farmers of the then new country at once turned their attention to the raising of grain, hay and vegetables to the extent of their ability, still it was not until four years later that a supply sufficient for the wants of the population could be produced at home. The production of grain was greatly retarded, owing to the difficulty experienced by the farmers in procuring seed and the myriads of grasshoppers that swarmed into the valleys and consumed every spear of grain before it was fairly headed out. So that with the exception of those who had engaged in raising potatoes and other vegetables and in cutting wild grass for hay, which sold at fabulous prices, very little was accomplished in the matter of irrigation until 1864. At that time the streams were all full until late in the season, and very few large ditches or canals were constructed, but those engaged in the business contented themselves with what might be termed high water ditches, that seldom exceeded a mile in length. From this small beginning the agricultural industry has grown, so that at present there are 536 farms, containing an acreage of 166,812, of which 143,409 acres are under fence and nearly all supplied with water ditches for irrigation. In many instances these ditches are owned by individual farmers. They vary in capacity from 25 to 250 inches and the length varies from one to five miles. In other cases several farmers have associated themselves together and constructed canals from five to twenty miles in length to convey water to their lands along the line. The Madison river, which has its source high up in the fire holes of the National Park, west of the Yellowstone lake, has the largest surplus of unappropriated water of any stream in that county, and whilst there are a large number of farms in the valley under irrigation, still few farmers use the waters of the main stream, but have appropriated the waters of tributaries flowing in from either side. On the eastern side, where the largest body of agricultural land is situated, the waters of the Jordan, Jack, Cedar, Bear, Indian, Wolf, Moose and Squaw creeks are largely used for irrigation, and on the west side are Horse, Ruby, Cherry, Wigwam, Moores and Spring creeks. A great portion of each are appropriated. One of the largest canals in the county is that from Spring creek, which is twenty-three miles in length, is about eight feet by six and two feet deep, and conveys the waters of Spring creek to the table lands south of Meadow creek, and land, where a few years since nothing but cactus would grow, is now producing large crops of grain, alfalfa and timothy hay. The early settlers as a general thing took up what seemed to them the most desirable hay lands, giving less attention to agriculture, and where their attention was given to the subject, failed to produce as good results as have since been attained on the grease wood and sage brush land, as the soil of the former contained more alkali, and the inexperienced grangers knew but little how to eradicate it.

On the Ruby valley for a distance of fifty miles in length, and varying from three to ten miles in width, the greater portion is under irrigation. On either bank ditch after ditch and canal after canal are constructed, and the waters of the main stream, as well as those of Wisconsin, Indian and Mill creeks, Ramshorn river, Alder, Idaho and Greenhorn gulches on the east, with Ledford, Robb, Sweetwater, Garden and Hinch creeks and Silver Springs on the west, the waters of the whole are utilized to their full capacity. Until storage reservoirs are constructed we are of the opinion that f large canals constructed on each side of the stream and the smaller ditches abandoned, there would be a great saving of water from seepage and evaporation. It would certainly be more easily handled and we think produce better results than are now obtained and much expensive and vexatious litigation would be avoided.

The Beaverhead valley, from the Beaverhead rock north some

fifteen miles, was settled early, and many of the settlers engaged in stock growing, but all had their gardens, grain fields and wild meadow lands, upon which they constructed ditches and irrigation mains. No great effort was put forth towards the reclamation of arid lands on the upper Beaverhead until the advent of the Utah & Northern Railway and markets were opened with Glendale, Butte and Anaconda for farm products, at which time the subject of irrigation received a great impetus, and several large canals were constructed and the waters diverted to such an extent that in dry seasons the bed of the stream is practically dry from Dillon north to its confluence with the Big Hole river and forming the Jefferson river.

The Beaverhead river, with Red Rock one of its principal tributaries, is perhaps the longest branch of the Missouri, having its source in the southern part of Madison County, in and around Red Rock lake, near the Idaho line, running thence in a westerly direction, throwing a broad loop into Beaverhead County, and, after a journey of 100 miles, returns again to Madison County. A few miles below the Red Rock lake, in what is called Centennial valley, is a point where the solid rock ledges approach from either side. Here is one of the most favorable locations for a storage reservoir in the State. The stream from the lake to this point is very flat, and a dam could be easily constructed that would back the water up into the lake. This point was selected by the engineers of Major Powell as the most desirable site on the stream, and the lands on each side of the river and around the marshy lake were withdrawn from entry so as not to interfere with the storage of water. A small appropriation by Congress for the erection of a storage reservoir at this place would be of inestimable value, as there are yet many thousands of acres of arid lands that could be reclaimed from that source alone, and cannot be successfully irrigated in any other way. The Big Hole river produces more water than either the Ruby or Beaverhead. It has but little irrigable lands as compared with the other streams, as it runs through canyons and narrow valleys until within ten miles of where it is joined by the Beaverhead and Ruby, forming the Jefferson river. Several large canals are completed, and the waters are used on the level valley between the rivers. On the Jefferson valley quite a number of large canals are already completed and in use, whilst others are in course of construction on both sides of the river, from Silver Star northward. At Waterloo is a fine, prosperous community that, in addition to the waters of Spring creek, have a canal from the Jefferson about twelve miles in length, and are engaged in the construction of another and longer canal. There is still a large amount of unappropriated water in the Jefferson river, which courses through and forms the north line of Madison County for a distance of forty miles, receiving the waters of Fish creek, the North and South Boulder rivers and several other smaller streams. From the South

Boulder a large amount of water for irrigation and placer mining has been appropriated. The waters of North and South Willow creeks are largely appropriated, so that during dry seasons but little if any runs to waste. The same may be said of Norwegian and Hot Spring, Cherry and Pole creeks, also South Meadow and Leonard creeks. North Meadow is a larger stream than either of the last named, but at the low stage of water but little remains unappropriated, and there are several small lakes on this stream that attempts have been made to improve for the purpose of storing water. There are large placers at and about Washington bar, where the waters of this stream are used before it reaches the valley for general irrigation purposes. There are, according to reports at hand, nearly 600 miles of ditches and canals in Madison County in the aggregate, with a capacity of about 150,000 inches of water, and, as heretofore stated, until storage reservoirs are constructed, no surplus in any of the streams except a small amount in Big Hole, a still larger amount in the Jefferson, and the largest amount of any single stream in the Madison river.

R. O. HICKMAN.

MISSOULA COUNTY.

I have been unable to secure complete statistics relating to the subject of irrigation in the County of Missoula, and am at a loss somewhat as to how to formulate a satisfactory report. I know of at this time but three or four irrigation schemes on what is anything like an extensive plan, or idea. One of these is the Republican Ditch Company, taking water out of the Skalkaho creek and Bitter Root river. The ditch perhaps in its greatest length is about twelve or fifteen miles, carries about 2,000 inches of water and irrigates 5,000 acres of land, possibly more. It is a joint stock company, the ownership of which is largely held by Marcus Daly, and very much of the water is used by him on his extensive farm at Riverside, in this county. The remainder of the stock is held by the neighboring farmers, who use the water of the ditch in their various farming projects.

The Surprise Ditch Company takes water from the Bitter Root river, its greatest length being fifteen miles. It also passes through the Daly ranch. More or less of the stock of this company is also held by Mr. Daly, the remainder by quite a considerable number of Bitter Root farmers, among others being Cortez Goff. This ditch, perhaps, furnishes water for two or three thousand acres. Then there is the Ætna Ditch Company, also taking water out of the Bitter Root river, the water from which irrigates perhaps 1,000 acres. The leading spirit in this last ditch is L. Frankton Warner.

There are an innumerable number of lesser irrigation schemes and individual water appropriations, taking in fact all of the waters of

Skalkaho creek, Willow creek, Girds creek, Burnt Fork, Three-Mile, Eight-Mile, Sleeping Child, Tin Cup, Grant creek, Rattlesnake, Lavalla creek, O'Keefe creek, Lynch creek and some of the waters of Lo Lo. There is also a company organized, composed principally of citizens of the city of Missoula, known as the Canon Ditch Company. It has now under construction and rapidly approaching completion a ditch taking the waters of the Hell Gate or Missoula river about five miles up the river from the city of Missoula, crossing the farm of Daniel E. Bandmann, coming out of the canyon on the south side of the river, thence following along the foot of the mountain with laterals, reaching to various tracts of land on the south side of the Missoula river. This project reclaims several hundred acres heretofore desert lands. It is expected to be made available for making the yards, lawns and orchards of South Missoula grow and blossom as a rose. It is estimated that this ditch will carry between four and five thousand inches of water, and the cost will be about $30,000. Its proprietorship is composed largely of the owners of the land on the south side of the Missoula river at Missoula.

I might add that there is a vast quantity of land in Missoula County now desert that could be reclaimed, but the expenditure necessary is greater than the individual farmers, or even a collection of farmers, could undertake; but a magnificent field is presented to the enterprising capitalist, as there is in our mountain streams, rivers and lakes a vast quantity of water, that by the expenditure of what would not to a man of means be a very considerable amount of money, could be used for the purpose of reclaiming this large tract of arid or desert lands, and the returns on the investment would be very large.

Missoula valley is exceedingly fertile and the county is peopled with quite an enterprising, frugal and industrious people, who, however, have not been able financially to cope with the physical conditions, have made the lands yield abundant harvest of fruit, grain, hay and all kinds of vegetables. A. G. ENGLAND.

MEAGHER COUNTY.

The situation in Meagher County as regards this problem of irrigation may be gathered with reasonable correctness from a few facts that I shall be able to give you. The Assessor of Meagher County reports for the present year 333 farms. These farms are none of them less in extent than 160 acres, many of them much larger, the average being over 500 acres. They all need irrigation to make them productive.

Our agricultural lands, and in that term I include all lands that, with water for irrigation, will produce crops, are confined principally to three large valleys: The Missouri valley, extending from Canyon Ferry southerly some forty miles to the southwest corner of the county, and embracing some 102,400 acres. The Smith River valley, extending from about ten miles south of White Sulphur Springs to old Fort Logan, some thirty-five or forty miles north, embracing 96,000 acres. The Musselshell valley, extending from its forks easterly about sixty miles, embracing 192,000 acres, making a total of 390,400 acres. Of this area 27,000 acres (about) are cultivated, leaving 363,400 acres of arid lands within our boundaries. About all cheap sources of water supply have been exhausted. All the water flowing during the irrigating season in the streams of the valleys I have named has been appropriated.

The ditches used are mostly small, constructed for single farms. In the Missouri valley several large ditches from the Missouri river supply each from four to ten ranches. A canal has been projected in the Missouri valley that directly and indirectly will reclaim from 8,000 to 10,000 acres. The stock is mostly subscribed, and it is hoped to commence the work of construction the coming spring. The opportunities for improving our present condition would seem to be by the construction of reservoirs in each of these valleys. Sites favorable for their construction are found in each, and the flow of water in the streams now appropriated for irrigating purposes is sufficient, if held in check by reservoirs through that season of the year when not used by the farmer, to nearly if not quite supply the entire area of agricultural land. J. E. KANOUSE.

PARK COUNTY.

I am not very well posted in regard to what has been done in the western portion of our county, but will give you what I know about the water and irrigation in my district. I can answer a great many questions in a few words. With water we can raise anything that could be expected in this latitude, and without water nothing. As for the supply of water, there is plenty for all the arid lands in this vicinity if it was properly handled and stored. I will first mention the Big Timber creek. This water could be stored with a very good reservoir site, and then it could be taken out with a small expense and thrown over into Otter creek, where there is a great deal of good agricultural land. Then comes the Sweet Grass, which throws a large amount of water in June and July. There could be a canal taken out of this stream and carried on the edge between Sweet Grass lake basin and White Beaver basin, where it could be distributed so it would supply all the arid lands in those places, and also supply the present demand on the Sweet Grass, and do away with all the present ditches now in use and under construction. Nature never formed a better reservoir site than on the Sweet Grass. A dam eighty feet high and not to exceed one hundred yards in length on top, would store a body of water averaging one mile wide and five miles long, and from fifty to eighty feet in depth, and covering no arid land whatever. Then the waters of Sweet Grass would supply hundreds of farms and increase our population 500 per cent.

As for the work that has been done, it is all the work of the farmers and stock men, who have combined together and taken out such ditches as would supply their own wants. There are twelve or fifteen ditches now taken out of the Sweet Grass, carrying from 200 to 1,200 inches, and I would venture to say in June and July 25,000 inches runs to waste. There is plenty of land on which to utilize it all if it was properly distributed. There is a great deal of land lying dormant along the Yellowstone, which all could be covered, but it will take large capital. Nowhere in Montana have I seen a section where water could be stored and utilized as cheap as in Big Timber and the Sweet Grass. W. A. HARRISON.

Sweet Grass.

SILVER BOW COUNTY.

Hon. W. A. Clark, of Butte City, to whom was delegated by the late State Irrigation Convention the task of preparing a statement showing the status of irrigation in Silver Bow County, was unexpectedly called east. In his stead I am invited to make some statement in reference thereto.

It is well known to every one residing within the State that this county is geographically located in the southwestern portion of Montana and on and along the western slope of the main range of the Rocky Mountains. Being the smallest county in area in the State, with an average altitude of over 5,000 feet, it is not surprising that it should contain less than a township of arable land, and being so high up in the mountains what little it has is pretty generally reclaimed by independent private enterprise. It has, however, valuable reservoir sites, where, by proper engineering development, large storage of water could be had and used for the benefit of Deer Lodge valley, if it could be spared here and should ever become necessary. The great uses of our water supply will be its storage and distribution in the upbuilding of manufacturing and reduction industries tributary to Butte City.

However much our water might be of benefit to its natural uses in agricultural lines, and however much of it the skill of intelligent engineering may develop for us, the great demand in the direction I have indicated will make it stand to us in value next to the commodities of gold, silver and copper. The ruling valuable component parts that go to make up the source of Silver Bow County's prosperity is labor, gold, silver, copper, water and fuel. In all of these items we are peculiarly interested, and in our economic system each is interdependent on the other. When, in simple truth, we recite that in fifteen years the life of Butte City as an ore producing center, by reason of our recovering from the earth gold, silver and copper, the world has been made richer in a sum greater than $200,000,000, and when we further state, without the fear of successful contradiction, that this calendar year of 1892 will add, of these materials, a value of over $30,000,000, with evidences of an annual increase as years roll by, and when the character of our low grade ores is considered, requiring for its dressing the primary element of water, then conceding to us the great growth of manufactories already on every hand, and the great industries to come, we may well say that we have no water to spare for irrigation in the sense of reclaiming arid lands.

Notwithstanding all of this, and for the very reason of this, we, of Silver Bow County, are greatly interested in the reclamation by irrigation of the great arable plateaus of Eastern and Northern Montana. We say to you that we are the great consumer of the results of the husbandry of Montana, and may for that reason, if no other, be counted upon to take a great interest in all questions relating to reclaiming the arid lands of the State of Montana.

Whether that reclamation is undertaken by the State or United States matters to us of Silver Bow County only as to which is determined to be the best agency. That it should be undertaken by one or the other immediately is seemingly an impending necessity.

GEO. W. IRVINE II.

YELLOWSTONE COUNTY.

Yellowstone County has an area of 3,390 square miles, and an estimated irrigable area of 500,000 acres. Its northern and southern boundaries are respectively the Musselshell and Yellowstone rivers, which constitute also its ample sources of water for irrigation.

As the Musselshell has its heads among mountains of low altitude, the melting snows by which it is fed become exhausted early in the season and its waters consequently fail when most needed. For the reclamation of the drainage basin of the Musselshell resort must be had, therefore, to storage reservoirs in which the spring freshets may be impounded until needed.

The Yellowstone river, on the other hand, heading as it does among the perpetual snows, rolls down its floods during the months of greatest heat and when the thirsty earth is in greatest need. The volume of the Yellowstone during hot weather is estimated at 4,000,000 miners' inches, which for practical irrigation could by means of storage reservoirs be greatly increased. The hydrographic basin of the Yellowstone, with interruptions, is about 400 miles long, and, including the adjacent mesas, reclaimable by high-line ditches, it has an average width of from eight to twelve miles. Expert estimates place the irrigable area of the entire Yellowstone basin as high as 8,000,000 acres. The capacity of the Yellowstone, conserved by storage, may therefore be regarded as ample for the most exacting droughts which are likely ever to be made upon it. The fall of the Yellowstone is so rapid that it offers especial facilities for the conducting of water onto the adjacent plateaus, and the time is probably not far distant when large areas of table-land which are now utilized only as ranges for cattle and sheep will be dotted with farm houses surrounded by fragrant orchards and by waving fields of green and gold.

Yellowstone is one of the youngest counties of the State. Its settlement practically dates from the advent of the Northern Pacific Railroad into Eastern Montana, in 1882. Adverse influences, which it is unnecessary to explain in this connection, have greatly retarded its agricultural development. Enough has been done, however, to demonstrate that in all-round capacity for production Yellowstone is second to no county in the State.

Aside from a few small ditches on the Musselshell, the principal development has been in Clark's Fork Bottom, a name applied to an enlargement of the valley of the Yellowstone, reaching westward from Billings for thirty miles. The ditches of this bottom aggregate perhaps 12,000 miners' inches, the largest of them having a nominal capacity of 5,000 inches and a length of thirty-nine miles. The area of Clark's Fork Bottom is nearly 60,000 acres.

The soil of Yellowstone County grades from a light sandy loam to heavy clay loam, clay loam of moderate weight predominating, and it is admirably adapted to the growth of grapes and cereals. Oats rarely weigh less than forty pounds per measured bushel, and yield from forty to eighty bushels to the acre, according to the skill of the cultivator. Wheat readily yields from twenty-five to forty bushels per acre, and owing to our comparatively low altitude, 3,100 feet, and our hot summers, hardens so perfectly as to have been pronounced by experienced Eastern millers to be equal, if not superior for flouring purposes, to the choicest Dakota No. 1 hard wheat. Our barley fully sustains the reputation of the State for the production of this cereal in exceptional quality. Dent corn grows here as well as in Northern Ohio; while potatoes, squashes, melons and vegetables in general, as elsewhere in the State, for size and quality trench upon the marvelous.

Of the hay-producing grasses, bluestem has been its habitat, and attains its highest perfection; but as it degenerates eventually under irrigation, timothy is being substituted gradually, and yields from two to three tons to the acre. In respect to alfalfa, Yellowstone is easily the banner county of the State. This marvelous plant thrives on all our soils, but especially on the sandy loam. With but a single irrigation after each cutting it yields three full crops yearly, aggregating from five to six tons per acre, of a hay so rich in nutritive value that it will make mutton or beef during a Montana winter, with the help only of shelter and water. All the small fruits, including grapes of medium season, grow luxuriantly. The hardier varieties of plums and of standard apples also do well.

Yellowstone County offers exceptional inducements to thrifty, intelligent farmers seeking homes. The best unimproved lands may be had here, under ditch, at from ten to fifteen dollars per acre, and under irrigation excellent crops can be taken from the sod within four months from the time it is broken. No county in the State is susceptible of more varied farming. The facility with which barley, peas, alfalfa, Hubbard squashes and corn can be raised affords the finest possibilities in dairying and in the making of hams and bacon, two industries scarcely represented in the county. Alfalfa is peerless for bee-farming and for poultry raising, while the making of beef and mutton from alfalfa, both green and dry, is destined to become a leading industry of the farmers of Yellowstone County and to add thousands to their wealth. Yellowstone County is without a flouring mill, and a fortune awaits the man who shall first build one here. Cheese and beet-sugar manufactories could command here the best of working material and an appreciative market.

Winter commences in Yellowstone County with great regularity during the closing days of December, and breaks in from two to six weeks. The chinook begins in February, and the 5th of March usually finds the farmer putting in his seed. The summers are long and hot.

A fact of immense practical importance to the future of Yellowstone County is the assurance of the sustained fertility of its lands. During the summer months the waters of the Yellowstone are thick with silt, the fertilizing wealth of the mountains from which they flow. The process of irrigation distributes this soil-laden water over the luxuriant fields, supplying their waste and quenching their thirst as from the fountain of perpetual youth. So that bountiful harvests suggest to the farmer no disquieting fears of the exhaustion of his soil, but rather remind him of his debt to that kindly Providence who by wonderful provision has thus ordained that by giving his fields shall not be impoverished, and that by the lapse of the years their natural force shall not be abated.   B. F. SHUART.

BILLINGS, Jan. 23, 1892.

ST. MARY'S LAKE COUNTRY.

It was my fortune to be able to visit the northwestern portion of the State east of the Rocky Mountains during the past autumn season. The purposes of my visit were an examination of the soil, nature of the country, and the possibilities of irrigation. Almost uniformly the soil on the eastern slope of the Rocky Mountains, to the Missouri river, is of an excellent quality, and produces a vigorous growth of native grass. A portion of it still being, and all of it having been until recently, included in an Indian reservation, but little is as yet known as to its adaptability for growing domestic products. I would like to say in this connection, however, that I saw here what I never saw before—flax of excellent quality growing native and wild, indiginous to the country. Also in several places I found native timothy growing, making a very excellent grass. Several streams have their origin in the Rocky Mountains, flowing eastward, and convey more or less water to the Missouri river. Chief among these are the Teton, the Marias and the Milk rivers, with their smaller tributaries. It is a noticeable feature of them all that in crossing over a strip of land somewhat irregular but probably fifty miles in width, all of them part with more or less of their water, and actually carry less water when emptying into the Missouri river than is found in them nearer to their source. This fact may possibly have connection with the artesian flow of water so generally found further down on the eastern slope. All of these streams when leaving the mountains are well defined and the flow continual, and carry considerable quantities of water. Their sources being so much above the general level of the country below, all of them can be taken from their native channel at varying expenses and conveyed over the lands below and used in converting into productive soil which would otherwise be uncertain in production for lack of moisture. Running in a northwesterly direction in the vicinity of the source of the Milk river is a high ridge which separates the chief source of that stream from the main range of the mountains. This state of affairs will account for the fact that late in the summer season but little water is found in the lower Milk river, because there is but one branch of that stream that has its origin in the Rocky Mountains.

Immediately behind this high ridge, and between it and the Rocky Mountains, lie the beautiful lakes known as St. Mary's lakes. The lower one of these lakes is about six miles in length, varying in width from one-quarter to one-half mile. The upper lake, which is about fifteen miles in length and somewhat wider than the lower one, lies further into the mountains, and is really the receptacle of nearly all the waters flowing into the two. The outlet of these lakes is the St. Mary's river, which runs in a northeasterly direction, following the north side of the high ridge above referred to. After a run of about ten miles it crosses the boundary into Canada. Emptying into St. Mary's river, about two miles below the lower lake, is the Swift Current, a stream about one-third the size of St. Mary's. This stream could easily be turned into the lower St. Mary's lake, thus increasing the volume of St. Mary's river about one-third where it leaves the lake. Within a mile or two of the Canadian boundary is a deep chasm in the high ridge above referred to. I am led to believe from the imperfect observations it was possible to make that the highest point within this chasm is considerably lower than the level of the water at the outlet of the lower lake. I am also led to believe that a careful survey would show that it were possible and feasible to take the waters out of St. Mary's river through the chasm referred to, and following the east side of the ridge formerly spoken of, crossing at the water level the various tributaries of the Milk river, adding these streams to the water in the ditch until the water could be brought out upon the high plain and distributed over the same.

The feasibility of the distribution I think is unquestionable, in view of the fact that there is a very perceptible incline in the whole country from the mountains east for several hundred miles. I am also led to believe that the large tributary of the Marias, known as the 'Cut Bank," could also be taken from its channel and made to join the waters of the St. Mary, and thus could be secured sufficient water to reclaim by irrigation at least 300,000 acres of excellent soil, which is otherwise unproductive for want of irrigation. The benefits that would be derived from such a vast reclaim of otherwise unproductive territory is in keeping with the magnitude of the undertaking. The possibilities of benefits to be thus derived are so great that it seems to me a matter well worth the consideration of Congress and justifying a suitable appropriation to determine whether such results are really possible. To ascertain this a topographical survey should be made. At present no person is sufficiently interested, otherwise than Congress, to justify the expense in making such a survey. A very trifling amount only would be required to ascertain whether the waters could be obtained in the manner indicated. If such were found to be true, then a more complete survey could be made. If it should transpire that it were not possible to carry the waters in the manner indicated, no further expense need be incurred. I am satisfied that here is the greatest opportunity now presenting itself in this State for Congress to do a great service to the State, and I sincerely believe you will be entirely justified in calling the attention of Congress to this matter by urging action on its part necessary to determine the true situation of the case. J. BOOKWALTER.

MISCELLANEOUS COMMENTS.

At the special request of Senator T. C. Power the following is printed.

NEW DEPARTURE MINES, BEAVERHEAD CO., MONT.
FEBRUARY 20th, 1892.

Senator T. C. Power, Senate Chamber, Washington, D. C.:

DEAR SIR: I am glad to learn that you have so far recovered from your late illness as to resume your seat in the Senate. I feel now as if I am justified in writing you what I have intended to write ever since the adjournment of the "Arid Land Convention," at Helena. Allow me to congratulate you on the stand you have taken on the arid land question. It is the only tenable one for us, in my judgment. The government owes it to the whole people to reclaim these lands and make them fit for cultivation and habitation. To cede them to the states and territories is to give to them the bone after the flesh has been taken from it. Those favoring the cession say sell the lands and with the proceeds reclaim them. Who would buy them? Not one section to-day could be sold individually or separately were they ceded. To sell them would bring us back to your idea as expressed at Helena. Trusts and corporations only would eventually acquire these lands, and the people would be under their yoke and at their mercy. Much can be said against the cession of these lands. I fully endorse your course and it meets with my unqualified approbation.

Yours Truly, LAWRENCE A. BROWN.

In explaining his position on the arid land question, in the San Francisco *Chronicle*, Senator Power said:

I spoke only for my own State, where the people do not want arid lands thrust upon them. I cannot speak for California, because the conditions may be such that what is good for us might be bad for that State. My claim is that the plan to take the arid lands away from the Federal Government is the scheme of a few men, acting in conjunction with the railroads, to increase their holdings and place in their hands a supreme power that cannot be otherwise than vicious. More than that, a consummation of this big job would result in the organization of a giant political machine, that in far-reaching effect and unlimited possibilities would cause Tammany to appear as a pigmy.

For instance, in Montana there are 40,000,000 acres of unsurveyed arid lands; the railroads have 17,000,000 acres more. If this scheme should be carried out there is nothing to prevent these men from going to the railroad men, who are willing, and saying to them, "Here, we are mutually interested in this thing. We will pool our issues and combine our strength and elect a Governor who will be our creature. Thus we will control all appointments, and we will control all this land, as well as politics generally."

Now, do you see the immense power these men would have? I will show you more. To survey these lands in Montana alone would cost much more than a million dollars. Do you see the possibilities in that single little item? Now, to go further, Montana is forced to run into debt to survey its little school lands. To survey all these arid lands would pitch it head over heels in debt, and with a body of unscrupulous men in control it would never extricate itself. Then the State would be forced, just as any unsuccessful business man is forced to do with his goods, to virtually give the land away in order to realize enough to pay its indebtedness, and that is the point in the proceedings where these political bosses and unscrupulous conspirators would step in and for a song increase their holdings.

This is all feasible, and I charge that there is now a conspiracy afoot in which all those points have been considered and adopted. Of course the railroads are in it. The biggest man in the Salt Lake Convention, which swallowed the bait, hook and all, and the man who more than any other carried the scheme through, was the general land agent of the Southern and Central Pacific railroads. He absolutely joked the Convention into adopting his policy. In Montana we want the arid lands to be kept in control of the Government, and we want that Government to adopt some plan by which a portion of the land can be sold and the proceeds applied to the reclamation of the whole. We stand ready to adopt anything that is fair to all the people.

www.ingramcontent.com/pod-product-compliance
Lightning Source LLC
Chambersburg PA
CBHW020300090426
42735CB00009B/1162